CHURCH IS MORE THAN BODIES, BUCKS, AND BRICKS

Jeremy Myers

RedeemingPress.com

For my father, Bill Myers
who taught me that ministry is about three things:

Loving God
Loving God's Word
Loving God's People

TABLE OF CONTENTS

INTRODUCTION

Anything worth doing is worth doing poorly.
—G. K. Chesterton

The funny thing about book introductions is that there really is no such thing as a book introduction. At least, not from an author's perspective. From an author's perspective, an introduction is more like a conclusion.

If an author writes an introduction before the book is written, the author is only writing what they *think* the book will be about, even though they don't really know how the book will end up. Inevitably, the process of writing a book causes the imagined argument and thought flow of a book to change in the process of writing and so any introduction which is written before the book ends up getting discarded or radically changed. This is why most book introductions are written *after* the book has been completed, and therefore, is more like a conclusion than a true introduction.

Such is the case with this introduction. I am writing this book introduction over two years after I finished writing the content of this book. That makes this introduction not only a conclusion to what I have written, but also, at least in the case of this book, some sort of strange apology.

I am not apologizing for the tardiness of this book, but rather, for the content. In the process of preparing this book for publication, I had the opportunity to read over the manuscript several times for editing, typesetting, and proofreading purposes. As always, I discovered numerous grammatical and typographical mistakes (which I fixed), but undoubtedly missed several more. I apologize for any I might have missed, but this is not the main reason for my apology.

I apologize because of the weaknesses and flaws in the content and argumentation of this book. Since it was written over two years ago, my thinking has developed quite a bit in some areas, and as I read and re-read this book to prepare it for publication, I kept thinking, "I need to change this, add content here, include footnotes about this idea, explain that pertinent biblical passage here. Oh, and there are those three books I've been meaning to read on this subject. I bet they would help sharpen my thinking." And so on, and so on.

I did include some of these changes, but finally, I just gave up and decided that it would have to be good enough. Though some people miss the forest for the trees, I was on the verge of missing the forest for the leaves. Many theologians and writers fall into a similar trap.

I recently read that J. R. R. Tolkien was a writing perfectionist, and if it had not been for his friend, C. S. Lewis, encouraging Tolkien to publish his books despite all the flaws that Tolkien saw in them, we never would have had the privilege of reading *The Lord of the Rings* trilogy. So if you have enjoyed reading these fantastic books by Tolkien, you can thank Lewis.

But it is not just novelists who struggle with this. Bible scholars and theologians deal with this difficulty as well. Several years ago when I was working as an editor for a publishing company in Texas, we were working on putting out a two-volume commentary on the New Testament. One of our contributors kept missing the deadlines for his portion of the commentary. Every time I called him, he was tracking down some new lead about a particular theological topic, or headed to the library to find an old journal article that he had read about in a footnote of some book, or was researching the semantic field of some Greek word. I kept telling him, "Look, you've missed your deadline ... again. Send it what you've got. It will have to be good enough."

He never sent anything in. His commentary was never quite ready. It was never quite good enough for submission (in his mind).

Finally, we had to cancel his publishing contract and get somebody else to write the commentary on his portion of Scripture. The volumes are now published, and he is not a contributor. The last I heard, he had decided to publish his commentary by himself, though according to him, it was still nowhere near complete. Honestly, I hope he completes it, because it will undoubtedly be one of the best and most comprehensive commentaries in existence on that book of the Bible. Yet if history is any guide, his commentary will never be done, for there will always be one more idea to look into, one more journal article to read, one more Greek word to research.

If something is worth doing, at some point you just have to do it, even if the final result is not as good as it could have been. G. K. Chesterton once said, "Anything worth doing is worth doing poorly." Certainly, we should always try our best and perform quality work, but Chesterton is absolutely right: If something needs to be done, it is better to do it poorly than to not do it at all. Sometimes, the quest for quality gets in the way of accomplishing anything significant.

Why have I taken this long rabbit trail as part of the introduction/conclusion to this book? Because the following chapters are hardly a "finished product." Despite all I write in this book about evangelism, tithing, and church buildings, there is a vast amount of information I wish I had included. Along with what I have written, there is much more that should have and could have been said.

Yet I felt that rather than put the project off indefinitely as I tried to find the time to include more information, more research, and more detail, it would be better to simply get something out there than to continue to put it off until I was completely happy with the finished product. Such is the writing life.

Let me take the point one step further and explain that everything I have written in this "Introduction" is not actually about writing at all. Why have I written this long rabbit trail about writing? Because it serves as an illustration, not about writing, but about church.

Church is one of those things that is worth doing, which means that it is worth doing poorly. If we wait until we have all our questions answered, every biblical passage about church properly understood, and everyone in agreement about the "best" way to be the church in the world, we will never get around to actually doing church.

So although the following chapters criticize three key elements of the way some Christians "do church," please do not read my criticism as condemnation. All I am really doing is asking some questions that many others are asking, and making a few suggestions about how church could be done differently.

Though the church is worth doing, and therefore worth doing poorly, this doesn't mean there isn't also room for improvement. The three suggestions in this book provide some ideas for ways to improve.

Ultimately, my primary concern is that no matter how you "do church," you at least somehow live and function as the Body of Christ in the world. My ultimate goal is that you follow Jesus into the world, however that may look. I think there may be some ways of following Jesus that work better than others and are more true to our calling to be the hands and feet of Christ in this world. You may disagree. But either way, I hope we can both celebrate the other person's desire to follow Jesus however and wherever He leads.

My desire for you as you read this book is that you ask the hard questions about how you do church, and whether or not there might be better ways to do church so that you can look more like Jesus and love others like Jesus in all you say and do. If you believe that your current method of doing church needs no improvement and is the best way to accomplish what Jesus has called you to be and do in this world, then by all means, continue down the path you are on. But if you have sensed a desire to implement a few tweaks to how you are following Jesus, or an increasing sense of something wrong with the way church is being done, then my hope and prayer is that this book will show you that such thoughts are not wrong or sinful, but may actually be Jesus calling you to follow Him outside the four walls of "Churchianity" and into a vibrant and daily walk with Him as He shows you how to be the church without bodies, bucks, or bricks.

1

ENOUGH WITH EVANGELISM

*To those in the West, the bigger the number
of respondents, the more replicated the
technique. The bigger the statistic, the greater
the success. Westerners are enamored by size,
largesse, number of hands raised, and so on.
When the sun has set on these reports, we seem
rather dismayed when statistics show the quality of life of the believer is no different from
that of the unbeliever. —Ravi Zacharias*

When you think of evangelism, what is it you picture? If
you are like most people, you probably imagine various activities, including going door-to-door to invite people to church,
standing on a street corner passing out tracts, or taking friends
and neighbors to an evangelistic crusade to hear an evangelist
present the gospel.

Notice that in all of these scenarios, evangelism is equivalent to talking. Preachers give evangelistic sermons where they

tell people about the gospel, evangelists go out to street corners and pass out gospel tracts while shouting Scriptures through a bull horn, or Christians walk around a neighborhood, knocking on doors to tell others about Jesus.

Statistics have shown that none of these forms of evangelism are particularly successful or helpful, and more often than not, give Christians a bad reputation as being little more than religious salesman.

This is why I say, "Enough with Evangelism!" Or at least, enough with *this kind* of evangelism.

I am all for evangelism, but not for the kind which does little more than inundate people with words upon words. In the following chapter, I will issue a call to cancel several word-heavy evangelistic approaches in exchange for a way of life that lives and shares the gospel in a tangible way with others.

But first, let me provide a little background about the activity of evangelism itself.

EVANGELISM: THEN AND NOW

I admit it: many of the evangelistic events we read about in the Gospels and Acts by Jesus and the Apostles were heavy on words. There is no denying it. Certainly, the evangelistic words of Jesus and the apostles were nearly always preceded or accompanied by acts of service and love, but there were usually a fair number of words involved in the gospel presentation as well.

On this basis alone, I would suggest that if a church or group of people wants to engage in words-based evangelism, they should seek at least to follow the example of Jesus and the apostles in balancing their words with acts of love, kindness, and service toward those they are seeking to reach. Going door-to-door or handing out tracts on the street corner accomplishes little and looks nothing like Jesus.

Nevertheless, there is a big difference that must not be overlooked between the time and area in which Jesus and apostles ministered and the time and area in which we now live.

The early message of the church was so revolutionary and hopeful, that it rarely took much more to get people's attention than to proclaim, "Jesus is Lord!" In the Roman Empire, Roman Citizens were required to confess that "Caesar is Lord." In such a setting, to say instead that "Jesus is Lord" would be interpreted by many as an act of treason against Caesar and the Roman Empire. Yet for those who were tired of oppression and abuse from the Roman government, such a cry was filled with hope for change and deliverance.[1]

But today, if you go into a shopping mall and shout, "Jesus is Lord!" nobody will even turn their heads. They my think you are a religious lunatic, but nobody will think you are shouting treasonous words, much less a message of hope, change, and deliverance. In his book, *Naming the Powers,* Walter Wink writes that "Jesus is Lord" bumper stickers mainly occasion yawns.

> Cars adorned with them are not stopped by police road-blocks or firebombed by paramilitary saboteurs. The only people scandalized by the phrase are those who regard its language as sexist. But there are countries where "Jesus, friend of the poor" can get you killed.[2]

It is obvious then, that even when it comes to the most basic words of the gospel—Jesus is Lord—we live in a different culture and a different time than what is recorded in Scripture. Even when we share the central truth of the gospel—that Jesus

---

[1] See, for example, Scot McKnight and Joseph B. Modica, eds., *Jesus is Lord, Caesar is Not: Evaluating Empire in New Testament Studies* (Downers Grove: IVP, 2013).

[2] Walter Wink, *Naming the Powers: The Language of Power in the New Testament* (Philadelphia: Fortress, 1984), 111.

gives eternal life to anyone who simply and only believes in Him for it—such words usually lack the shock value that the same words would have had in the first century Mediterranean world.

It seems then, that modern day evangelism must not seek to simply share the same words that were shared in the first century world, but share them in such a way that causes people to sit up and take notice. The gospel is not just a bunch of words, but also involves sharing and showing the truth of those words in such a way that shocks people into considering what sort of impact those words would have on their life if they were to believe them.

When it comes to evangelism, words alone are no longer enough. In fact, as we will see later, sharing the gospel by words alone is not even biblical. But I am getting ahead of myself.

DESTINATION-BASED EVANGELISM

The main problem with evangelism today is that it seems to be focused primarily on a destination. We tell people that if they believe the gospel, they can go to heaven when they die, and while they wait for that to happen, they should attend our church on Sunday morning. The goal of the modern gospel, it seems, is to get people into pews while they wait to get into heaven. But neither goal is emphasized in any biblical presentation of the gospel.[3] Jesus and the apostles rarely (if ever) present the promise of heaven or the practice of attending church as the goal of the gospel.

Why then are such things emphasized so frequently today? Oh sure, pastors and evangelists mention things like the for-

---

[3] I would prefer to say that neither goal is *present* in any biblical presentation of the gospel, but I know that such a statement would require extensive exegetical proof, which is well beyond the scope of this book.

giveness of sin, and reconciliation with God and others as some of the benefits of believing the gospel, but if you were to ask the average non-believer who had just sat through a gospel presentation what benefits they would receive and what they were expected to do as a result of believing the gospel, the vast majority would say that there were promised entrance into heaven, and while they wait for that to occur, they are expected to attend church on Sunday morning. Usually, there is an emphasis on the latter. The basic thrust of many evangelistic messages is this: "If you believe the Gospel you will go to heaven, and while you wait, you must attend church."

If you ask the average person if they can go to heaven without ever attending church, most people—Christian and non-Christian alike—will say no, that if a person wants to go to heaven, then they must attend church. For most, the gospel message is a message about destinations: where you go when you die, and where you go while you live. In destination-based evangelism, we want to get people onto the membership rolls of our church and get their names written in the membership rolls of heaven.[4]

To see this in more detail, let us look at a few of the more popular evangelism strategies which focus on getting bodies into the pews while they wait for entrance into heaven. Following this brief look at a few popular evangelistic methods, we will consider what the goal of the gospel should be, and how we can present the gospel in a way that causes contemporary people to sit up and take notice, just as they did in the first century Roman Empire when the church went about proclaiming the treasonous declaration that "Jesus is Lord."

---

[4] You even sometimes hear pastors talk about a giant scoreboard in the sky that keeps track of how many people have believed the gospel, so that when the "full number of Gentiles has come in" (Rom 11:25), and the countdown clock reaches zero, the end of all things will come.

SELLING GOD ON THE STREET CORNER

One popular form of evangelism is street evangelism. I don't know why it is so popular, because of all forms of evangelism, it may be simultaneously the least effective and the most annoying. Probably it is popular because it feeds people's desire for attention, helps them feel pious and holy when they get mocked (they think of this as persecution), and they believe that this is the form of evangelism that Jesus and Paul used when they preached in the marketplaces and public gathering areas of the first century world. Of course, as we will see, there are modern equivalents to the methods of Jesus and Paul, but the equivalent is *not* standing on a street corner and yelling at people while you shove piles of literature into the hands of people who pass by.

Let us look first at how this sort of evangelism is often carried out today, before concluding with some suggestions for how it *could* be (and is) done today.

One popular form of evangelism is what I call Bullhorn Evangelism. This is when a person stands on a street corner, and shouts into a bullhorn at people who pass by. In more recent years, the bullhorn is sometimes replaced with a portable microphone and loudspeaker.

While it is true that some people receive eternal life through these sorts of street preachers, it is also true that for every one person who receives eternal life, hundreds more are turned off by such a presentation of Christ and Christianity. This is why such a method of evangelism is both the least effective form of evangelism in existence and also the most annoying. It accomplishes very little and at great cost to the cause of Christ.

When I was growing up, there was a street in town with lots of bars on it. A man named "Red" was a regular patron on this street. But although he was often surrounded by empty beer cans and other assorted trash, he never entered a bar and never had a drink. The bottles and cans were thrown at him by drunk

20

revelers. Why? Because every night he walked up and down the street, waving his Bible in the air and shouting his version of the gospel through a bullhorn. When people threw bottles and cans at him, Red loved it all the more, because he thought he was enduring persecution for the cause of Christ.

Looking back now, I wonder who was persecuting whom?

During my Junior year in High School, I went with a friend of mine, Jay Bradford, to interview Red on a Saturday night. We asked him why he kept preaching when clearly, people didn't want to hear his message. He said that he had the message of life, and people needed to hear it whether they wanted to or not.

We asked him how long he'd been preaching. He told us it had been seventeen years.

How many converts had he seen? His answer: Only eternity will tell.

But how many conversions was he personally aware of within the past year? One.

Yes. One.

Upon further discussion, it turned out that even this one had been drunk. He had come out of a bar late at night, staggering under the effect of alcohol, had thrown up in the street, and then, at the invitation of Red, had confessed his sins, asked to receive Christ, and then stumbled off into the night, never to be heard from again.

Nevertheless, Red was convinced that countless thousands of others had also received Jesus as a result of his street preaching. "Besides," he said, "It's my job to preach; it's God's job to save."

You can't argue with that.

Or can you?

This idea that "It's worth it if just one is saved" overlooks the fact that most often, to get one person saved using these methods, you turn thousands of people away who might have otherwise believed in Jesus if a different approach had been used. I don't think God is necessarily pleased by our evangelism strategies when we come to Him with one saved soul, when we could have come with 10,000 if we had only used different methods.

To put it another way, is it worth saving one person if, in the process of saving one, we present the gospel in a way that ensures that the thousands of people who hear our presentation of the gospel want nothing to do with Jesus for the rest of their lives? While it is true that our job is to preach and God's job is to save, it is often true that if we stopped preaching, God's job might be easier.

In college, I encountered another form of street preaching: the sandwich board preacher. I was attending the state university, and one day on my way to class, I noticed a large crowd gathering around a man with a sandwich sign strapped to his shoulders. Next to him stood a young girl, probably around ten years old, dressed all in white. I found out later this was his daughter.

It was the sign, however, that caught my eyes. In big, bold, burning, red letters across the top it read: "GOD HATES..." and then scattered around the rest of the board were groups of people that God hates: liars, cheaters, atheists, drunks, adulterers, and gays (he used a different word, which I won't include here).

He also had a bullhorn, and was busy announcing to the growing crowd of college students that all sinners were going to hell. He claimed that he had not sinned in 21 years, and his ten year-old daughter had never sinned in her entire life. Some Christians who were there tried to argue with him that the one who says they have not sinned is a liar (1 John 1:8). His response was that he wasn't claiming he had not sinned. He had. Twenty-one years ago. And his daughter wasn't claiming she had not sinned. He, the father, was making that claim. I can't be certain, but I don't think he got any "converts" that day, or even moved anybody in the right direction. So far, Red was up on this guy by one.

A year later, I found myself at Moody Bible Institute in Chicago. One of the classes I had to take was a course on evangelism. As part of the course, some of the students went out every weekend to do street evangelism. Every week in class they stood up to give share what God was doing through their efforts, and to invite all of us non-evangelizing students to join in. So one weekend, I went, not because I wanted to, but because I felt guilty for taking a class on evangelism without going into the streets to do any evangelism. (Have you ever noticed that guilt is a heavy motivator in evangelism—both in those who do it and in the message they preach? That should tell us something is wrong with evangelism.)

The approach these students used was a little more tasteful than that of Bullhorn-Evangelist Red or the college campus Sandwich-Board preacher. One student was a bit of an artist, and he set up a big easel on a corner of Michigan Avenue in Chicago, and proceeded to draw gospel-related images on the easel while preaching in a loud voice.

While he did that, the rest of us students acted as "crowd primers." It is normal street corner psychology that if a crowd is standing around watching something, you want to stop and see what is going on. So we "created the crowd." We were supposed to walk up as if we were normal people on the street, and then stop and watch him draw and listen to him preach. After a dozen or so students had "stopped to listen," other people would usually stop, watch, and listen as well. The guy talked and drew for about five minutes, and then, as he closed up, each of us in the crowd were supposed to pull a gospel tract out of our pocket and hand it to a stranger nearby before asking what they thought about Jesus and the message they had just heard, and if they had any questions or wanted us to pray with them.

I still remember feeling like we were setting a trap for people. It was even stranger because in my first attempt at this, there were about three students for every actual person. So when the presentation was over, each "unsaved" person got swarmed by three students handing them tracts and asking to pray with them. Imagine how they must have felt! They thought they were gathered with a bunch of other strangers on the sidewalk, only to find out that the vast majority of the crowd was fake bystanders just waiting to pounce on unsuspecting souls.

I don't think we got any converts that day, but if we did, I don't remember. I felt too dirty and ashamed to care. Some might say I was ashamed of the gospel, but I don't think that was it at all. I was not ashamed of the gospel, but was deeply ashamed of *how* we had tried to present the gospel. Looking back, I don't think that what we had done had much to do with the gospel at all.

There are numerous others forms of street evangelism, but they basically all share the same sort of message and approach, and more often than not, it seems that more damage is done to the cause of Christ and the gospel than any real, lasting good. Even when there are supposed "conversions" in such encounters, it is nearly impossible to perform any follow-up or discipleship with these converts, as usually, after they read your gospel tract and say a prayer, they continue on their way down the street, never to be heard from again.

So I am not a fan of any of these forms of street evangelism. They show nothing of the neighborly love or sacrificial service that are central to the biblical gospel. Granted, there's no telling what the Holy Spirit might do, or who He can use to bring people to Jesus, but whenever I encounter street preachers of the sort described above, I always wonder if there might be a better, more gentle, personal, and forgiving way of drawing people to Jesus Christ. As Nathan L. K. Bierma points out, such street-evangelism techniques seem "to have found the most alienating way to talk to people (or *at* people), the way that involves the least listening, the least smiling, the least humility, the least possibility of getting anything but a cold shoulder in return."[5]

There are, however, many who argue that the reason we should practice such forms of evangelism is because this is the method that Jesus, Peter, and Paul used in their gospel preaching. Street preachers often point out that Jesus, Paul, and others would go into the busy streets and marketplaces of towns and cities, and proclaim the good news to whomever they found there. This is true.

But what few people realize today is that such a method of spreading news was commonly practiced in the first century Roman Empire. They didn't have printing presses, newspapers, or even a postal system. So when merchants, philosophers, or government officials wanted to spread the news about something, they would stand in a busy area of town, or walk through the streets, shouting the news. This is how announcements and messages were commonly broadcast to the public in that time.

This, of course, it is not how news and announcements are spread today. Today, we use books, blogs, newspapers, social networking sites, television, radio, and email. So if a person wants to follow the example of Jesus, Peter, and Paul in broadcasting the gospel to strangers "on the street," the way to do this is modern society is not by literally preaching on the street, but by proclaiming the good news in the modern marketplaces and gatherings spots of our world, which is through publication, television, radio, and the internet.

---

[5] Nathan L. K. Bierma, *Bringing Heaven Down to Earth* (Phillipsburg, NJ: P&R, 2005), 136.

While there are people who shout on street corners and use psychological techniques to gather crowds in public places, they are usually only selling something or performing a show. Evangelists should not be confused with vendors and street performers, but when we shout on street corners, that is exactly how we are viewed: as someone trying to sell God or put on an amusing show for others.

But what about large-group evangelism? In the days of Jesus, Peter, and Paul, it seems that they had much success in preaching the good news to crowds who had gathered on hillsides, civic centers, or coliseums. Can similar methods be used today to proclaim the gospel to people? It seems there may be a place for this in today's culture since speaking to large audiences is a common occurrence in society today, such as with political rallies, entertainment venues, and speaking tours by popular and famous leaders. Might "crusade evangelists" make use of such venues to share the gospel? While I think that such an approach may be slightly better than bullhorn and door-to-door evangelism, I am still not convinced that crusade evangelism is the most effective way of sharing the gospel today.

NO MORE CRUSADES

Crusade evangelism is a strategy that has been used since the First Great Awakening in the mid-1700s. It began in England and America where popular preachers gathered together large crowds of people and preached the gospel to them. Some of the leading evangelists to use this strategy include D. L. Moody, George Whitefield, Jonathan Edwards, John Wesley, Charles Finney, and in more recent years, Billy Sunday, Billy Graham, Franklin Graham, Luis Palau, and Greg Laurie.

Without a doubt, millions of people around the world have heard the gospel and received eternal life as a result of these crusades. They are, and continue to be, a meaningful and effective way of spreading the good news about Jesus Christ.

Yet in a 1990 interview with PBS, Billy Graham himself stated his belief that only about 25% of those who come forward at one of his events actually became Christians. More recent studies have shown that only 6% of people who "come forward" at an evangelistic crusade are any different in their beliefs or behavior one year later. Of course, it is estimated that Billy Graham preached to more than 200 million people, and 6% of 200 million is still 12 million. That is not insignificant.

In recent decades, ministries that are involved in crusade evangelism have tried to increase the long-term effectiveness of their efforts by engaging local churches and ministries to perform follow-up discipleship with those who come forward at a crusade. They recognized that the Great Commission in Matthew 28:19-20 calls for discipleship, not just evangelism. The Great Commission calls for people to learn about Jesus and follow Him; not just pray a prayer or make a decision about Jesus. I applaud such a move by crusade ministries, and believe it is a step in the right direction.

But if crusade evangelists are taking a step in "the right direction," what is the direction they are stepping toward? I find it interesting that by seeking to get people who come forward involved in relationships with others people in the community, the crusade ministries are moving toward relational evangelism. They recognize that big tent, big event evangelism does not achieve the long-term results which comes only through long-term relationships with other people. Recognizing the failures of their approach to make disciples, they have tried to take the relational emphasis of interpersonal evangelism and tack it on to the tail end of their events. But this raises the question: if they recognize that relational evangelism is more effective, then why not dump crusade evangelism altogether, and just focus on training people to practice relational evangelism?

Sure, over the course of 50 years, Billy Graham may have helped 12 million people come to faith in Jesus and begin a life of discipleship to Him. But have you ever stopped to think about the hundreds of millions of dollars that were spent for those 12 million converts? The Billy Graham Evangelistic Association currently spends about $100 million per year. I wonder if there might be a more effective way of spending hundreds of millions of dollars for evangelistic purposes than evangelistic crusades? For example, studies say that relationship evangelism is the most effective form of evangelism. What would have happened if hundreds of millions of dollars were spent training and supporting relationship evangelists?

The estimates for the number of evangelical Christians in the world range from 300 million to 700 million. Let's just say that the Billy Graham Evangelistic Association had decided to spend their money on relational evangelism training instead of crusades, and that in 50 years of operation, they trained only 1% of the lower estimate of 300 million Christians worldwide, or 3 million Christians. Studies report that people who are trained in relational evangelism see about one friend, coworker, neighbor, or family member become a follower of Jesus every year. But let's err on the side of caution, and say it is only one every four years.

Now, let's take those 3 million Christians who have been trained in relational evangelism, and give them 50 years to develop relationships and help other people become followers of Jesus Christ. At an average rate of one person every four years, these 3 million Christians would see over 37 million people become followers of Jesus. Even with all of the low estimates, this is triple the results of Billy Graham! What is more, having helped lead a person to faith in Jesus Christ, these friends, neighbors, and relatives would still be around to help encourage, equip, and disciple the people who had become Christians. When relationship evangelism is practiced, relationship discipleship is not something tacked on at the end, but is inherent within the process.

I really dislike talking about numbers of converts this way, because evangelism is not about numbers. But the crusade evangelists are always talking about the numbers of people who have been reached through their ministries, and when the numbers are really crunched it becomes clear that much like the street evangelist preaching through a bullhorn, crusade evangelists have chosen a relatively ineffective method of reaching people for Jesus Christ. In a culture infatuated with glamor, lights, shows, and crowds, crusade evangelism makes more headlines than it does disciples.

But aside from the relative failure regarding the numbers of converts made and the amount of money spent, crusade evangelism is damaging in other ways as well.

For example, crusade evangelism is also coercive. I occasionally attend evangelism crusades myself, and I always get the uncomfortable feeling that people were coerced into converting. Many of the techniques used in crusade evangelism were learned from the fields of marketing, sales, entertainment, and group psychology. The carefully crafted appeals to come forward at a crusade are often emotional in nature, based on success stories of people who converted, or tales of woe about people who did not. Sometimes these stories contain vivid portrayals of heaven and hell, complete with promises that those who come forward can enjoy eternal bliss with God in heaven, while those who sit comfortably in their seats may suffer eternal torment in the flames and blackness of hell for all eternity.

I once saw a speaker at a teen rally ask all the high school students to write their names on a piece of paper. Then, up on stage he had two barrels. In one, he put fluffy cotton, a Bible, and some gold (fake, of course). In the other barrel, he started a raging fire. Then he told the kids to come forward and drop their name into the barrel which signified where they wanted to go when they died. They could choose heaven (the fluffy barrel) or hell (the fire barrel). Not surprisingly, this speaker was able to go home to his church and report that every single teenager at the teen rally had "made a decision for Christ."

This example is a bit extreme, but most strategies at evangelistic crusades are only slightly more subtle. First, we are told that God loves us and really wants to spend eternity with us. But there is a big problem: we are sinners. So instead of living with us for eternity, God has to send us to hell where we will burn and suffer unimaginably for ever and ever. If that doesn't sound like fun, then there is another option: you can receive Jesus Christ instead. Since He died on the cross and rose from the dead, we can now go back to spending eternity with God! If that sounds better than burning forever in hell, the listeners are invited to come forward while the band plays some nice music, and a counselor will be more than happy to speak with you and lead you in a prayer.

You see? It is essentially the barrel of fluff and barrel of fire approach, but without any actual flames.

Evangelists who use these techniques often feel justified in using them due in part to Christ's command in Luke 14:23 where the Master tells His servant to go to the highways and byways and *compel people to come in* that the house may be filled for the banquet which He has prepared. Crusade evangelists believe it is okay to use compelling and persuasive techniques to get people to come forward at an evangelistic event, if it results in the person saying a prayer or making a decision to follow Jesus.

In previous centuries, this same passage from Luke 14 was used by other pastors and church leaders to "persuade" people to convert to Christianity. Luke 14:23 was one of the verses used during the actual Crusades of the Middle Ages where armies of Christian soldiers swept over the Middle East to retake Jerusalem for Jesus Christ. Those soldiers who went to war in the name of Christ used the edge of the sword against their foes to "compel them to come in." The cry of "Convert or Die!" is not just a Muslim practice.

Crusade evangelists today may not use the edge of a sword, but many are known to use the cutting edge of technology and psychology to compel their listeners to come forward. Further still, while most Christians would not condone a "convert or die" message today, we nevertheless provide our full backing and support for the "turn or burn" message of much crusade evangelism. We don't kill people, but the sinister message is still the same: If you don't join us, you will suffer the consequences forever in hell. This is the message of crusade evangelism, whether we are talking about the Crusades of the Middle Ages or the Crusades of the Modern Ages.

Crusades were not helpful then, and they are not helpful now. Though in the Middle Ages, the Crusades coerced people into becoming Christians with sword point and steel, today we coerce people with Powerpoint and emotional appeal.[6] Coercion is still coercion, not matter what kind of crusade we undertake.

What about the people who truly do convert in these modern methods? I do not deny that there are millions of such conversions. Yet as briefly stated above, the lasting effect of these conversions is minimal at best. I wonder if part of this is not only the lack of ongoing discipleship of the new Christians, but also somewhat due to the *way* in which the people became Christians. By converting at an evangelistic crusade, what is the first thing we teach these people about Christianity and following Jesus? What theological ideas about God and church are we affirming?

The typical message at an evangelistic crusade follows this outline: God loves you, but you are a sinner. As a sinner, you

---

[6] For more on this subject, see Philip J. Lee, *Against the Protestant Gnostics* (New York: Oxford, 1987), 116-119, 164-165.

are alienated from God, and can do nothing to correct that alienation. If you continue in that state, you will suffer eternal alienation from God in everlasting hell. But God, out of His great love for us, created a way of escape from eternal punishment—you must be born again. There is little agreement among evangelists about the method of being born again, but the requirements often include raising a hand, coming forward, saying a prayer, signing a card, confessing Christ, repenting of sins, believing in Jesus, and getting baptized.

I am not saying that people are not saved with this approach. People are. What I saying, however, is that there are so many dangerous ideas within such an approach, it seems that those who convert do so in *spite* of the message, *not* because of it.

What sort of dangerous ideas are inherent within this message? It is hard to know where to begin.

The message preached in evangelistic crusades leaves out a huge portion of the gospel. The message is too otherworldly. It is a message about the afterlife only, about heaven and hell and what happens to us after we die. The message rarely has much application or relevance for life here on earth, unless it is some vague notion that God wants to help us with our needs if we will just pray, obey, and go to church. I understand that the evangelist can only say so much and that the message of eternal life is the most vital part of the gospel since it affects people's eternal destiny, and that the ministries encourage local churches to do the follow-up discipleship so that other truths of the gospel can be taught.

But this is exactly the problem. When a crusade evangelist gets all the glamor, glitz, and glory of presenting the "gospel" to a crowd of 50,000 people and the people hear a message about being born again, but then those who respond attend a church without all the glamor, glitz, and glory and they hear a message about discipleship, following Jesus, danger, famine, persecution, and suffering, they rightfully feel that somebody is not being honest. The requirements of discipleship are not what they signed up for. They signed up for the free gift of eternal life, the feeling of knowing that their sins were forgiven, and the rush of coming to Christ in front of vast hordes of people.

But when the church music is poor quality, the pastor's sermons drone on and on about things they don't understand, and there is no glory of standing in front of everyone, no emotional high every week, the people feel like they missed something, that maybe Christianity is fake, or it "didn't take," and they abandon church in droves. The only way the church can combat this, of course, is to maintain the glamor, glitz, and glory of the crusade evangelists while at the same time, dumbing down the gospel message and the requirements of discipleship. Many churches in recent decades have successfully accomplished such changes to their Sunday morning structure, which accounts for much of the rise of the modern mega church movement.

Again, most of this is not an issue with relational evangelism. When you develop a long-term friendship with someone, they see the struggles and challenges you face. They watch you deal with lost jobs, broken marriages, and moral failures. But through it all, they also observe your faith and commitment to following Jesus and serving others. It's not perfect. It's not glorious. But it's real. There are no jumbotrons and spotlights, but there are small acts of love. There are no daily news headlines, but there are daily commitments to faith and hope in God, even when God doesn't act like we think He should.

This brings up another problem with the popular message of crusade evangelism. The message of crusade evangelism is too transactional. The inherent message is that if we do certain things that God wants, such a go forward, say a prayer, or get baptized, then God will give us certain things, like eternal bliss and happiness. This message is not part of the gospel. Eternal life is a free gift of God to those who receive it, and many of the blessings and benefits of being a child of God are irrevocable. Where there are blessings and benefits which depend on our obedience, it is not as though God gives these things *in response* to our behavior, but that we simply *access* what He has already provided. Crusade evangelism gets this all mixed up from the very beginning, which somewhat explains why so many people believe that loves and blesses only those who can perform the proper works, but hates and curses those who do not. This is not the Gospel of God as revealed in Jesus Christ.

One final problem with crusade evangelism is that the message preached at these events is simply not biblical. By this, I do not mean that the primary ideas that the evangelist preaches cannot be found in Scripture. To a degree, they can. It is absolutely true that God loves us, and we are sinners, and the wages of sin is death, and eternal separation from God awaits those who do not receive eternal life. Notice, of course, that I did not include in this list the practice of saying a prayer, raising a hand, signing a card, coming forward, or other such crusade evangelism activities. None of these are found anywhere in Scripture. Eternal life is received by believing in Jesus for it, not by praying a prayer, walking an aisle, raising a hand, or signing a card.

But this is not the primary problem with the message preached at crusades. The primary problem is that the *rest* of the message is not biblical either. The main content of the typical evangelistic message cannot be found anywhere in the Bible. Sure, bits and pieces can be pulled from various places, but nowhere in Scripture do we find Jesus or an apostle preaching the entire "evangelistic" message to one group at one time in one place. Doesn't this seem curious? If the message preached at most evangelistic events truly is "the gospel" how is it that we do not find this message summarized anywhere in Scripture all together in one passage as it is preached in the typical crusade? The message preached at most evangelistic crusades can only be cobbled together by pulling from numerous texts in various contexts. This seems odd, does it not? How is it that we decided that *these points* and not some of the others in Scripture constitute "the gospel"? Who decided that *these* verses and not others were the essential message? And if this gospel we have cobbled together is the message which must be believed to be born again, why didn't God deem it necessary to include that message somewhere within the pages of Scripture for us?

Some would point to Romans, and say their message is all there. I do agree that all the points mentioned in the typical evangelistic sermon can be proof-texted from Romans. But in doing so, the evangelist must choose a verse or two from each of chapters 3, 5, 6, and 10 (Usually in this order: 3:10; 3:23; 5:12; 6:23; 5:8; 10:9-10). One wonders if Paul would agree that his letter to the Romans could accurately be summarized with this selection of verses. The more I study Romans, the more likely I think that such a selection of verses, rather than accurately representing Paul's argument, completely *distorts* the message Paul intended.

While we are on the subject of Paul's theology, it should be pointed out that 1 Corinthians 15 does not include the entire message typically shared at evangelistic crusades either. As with Romans, this passage comes close, but the evangelist must arbitrarily cut off Paul in mid-sentence at the end of verse 4, and then must also go to other Scriptures in other passages to get some of the other key points which the evangelist wants to make.

All of this leads me to believe that there is something not quite right with the message and methods of crusade evangelism. Can God use crusade evangelism to bring people into His kingdom? Of course! He can and He does. I just think that as effective as it is, there are better, more effective, and more faithful ways of living and teaching the gospel of Jesus Christ.

35

Ultimately, we see that this extremely popular form of evangelism has the goal of getting bodies into pews and souls into heaven, but not much is emphasized regarding the rest of the Gospel, which concerns the advancements of the rule and reign of God in people's lives and around the world here and now. Most crusade evangelists must submit annual reports to their supporters about the crowds of people they preached to and the numbers of people who "responded." So once again, it is not really about life-change or making disciples, but about using a cobbled gospel and psychological manipulation to pull together as many "bodies" as possible.

CONFRONTING CONFRONTATIONAL EVANGELISM

Another popular form of evangelism is what I call confrontational evangelism. Such methods purport to follow the way of the Master Evangelist, Jesus, by "using the law lawfully." How does one do this? Essentially, it involves getting people to admit that they are a sinner, and are therefore under the condemnation of a righteous God. Once people see that they stand as a condemned sinner before God, the idea is that they will then understand their need of a Savior, and will turn to Jesus Christ in response.

While I think there may be a place for this sort of approach, and I do think that Jesus, Peter, and Paul used similar methods in *some* of their evangelistic encounters (cf. Luke 18; Acts 2; Romans 2), I am not convinced that this is the *only* of evangelism, or even the best way.

Yet the way this form of evangelism is often presented gives the impression that it is the only way to present the Gospel. Those who follow this method often teach that unless a person understands and recognizes that they are a sinner who stands condemned before a holy God, that person will never believe in Jesus for eternal life. In my own evangelism experiences, I don't find this to be the case, but more importantly, I don't see Jesus, Peter, and Paul following this pattern in *every* evangelistic encounter of their own. More often than not, the gospel offer of Jesus, Peter, and Paul is not based on our failure to please and obey God, but rather, on the incredible blessings and benefits that God offers to humanity out of His great love for us.

The biggest problem of all with this method of evangelism, however, is its emphasis on judgment, hell, and the wrath of God. In all of the trainings I have ever attended on this form of evangelism, in all of the books I have ever read, and in all of the evangelism encounters I have ever witnessed, those who use this method of evangelism seem to beat people over the head with condemnation about their sin. They threaten people with spending eternity in a fiery hell, and make frequent mention of God's hatred toward sin and the wrath which will fall upon unrepentant sinners.

I find such an approach toward people to be exactly the opposite of Jesus' methods in the Gospels, and exactly the opposite of the evangelistic methods of the apostles. Despite the claims of people who use this method, Jesus does not talk about hell more than heaven, and does not talk about God's wrath more than God's love.[7]

Furthermore, from the theological and practical perspectives, consider what people hear when we evangelize by talking about hell. We are effectively saying this:

---

[7] The only way the claim can be made that Jesus talks about hell more than heaven is to think that all references to "outer darkness" and "weeping and gnashing of teeth" refer to hell. Such a view completely ignores the historical and cultural contexts of these texts, which reveal that the image of "weeping and gnashing of teeth" refers to the experience of some believers at the Judgment Seat of Christ (Matt 13:42; Luke 13:28). The phrase, "weeping and gnashing of teeth" is a symbolic way of writing about deep and profound regret.

> God loves you so much that He wants to have an eternal relationship with you. But if you don't want to have one with Him, He's going to punish you forever in hell.

That is an ominous and portrays a God that looks nothing like Jesus. What if I came up to you and said,

> I would love to be your friend. I want to hang out with you, and go to dinner and basketball games with you. It will be fun. And oh, by the way, if you don't reciprocate this desire, I will hunt you down and kill you.

Nobody would try to start a friendship this way, and yet this is what confrontational evangelism methods are essentially telling people. They say that although God loves them, if they don't love Him back and do what He says, then He expresses His love by torturing them forever in eternal flames. Ultimately then, confrontational evangelism methods involve judging and condemning people for their sins, followed by hitting them over the head with the baseball bat of hell, and then hoping that despite such spiritual and psychological abuse, they will want to have a relationship with God.

We must not try to threaten people into a relationship with God. This is not ever the way Jesus evangelized. The true way of the Master Evangelist Jesus is the way of service, friendship, generosity, self-sacrifice, forgiveness, grace, restoration, reconciliation, and love. Without such things, we are not following the way of Jesus.

> Rather than shooting at what one believes is wrong in another person's life or way of thinking, love looks for the best, looks for truth, and then builds upon it. A loving approach to evangelism finds an area of expressed need, un-

certainty, or longing and then seeks to meet it as Christ would.[8]

So I am not a fan of the various forms of confrontational evangelism. Such methods do not reflect the heart of God for people, nor do they reflect the way of Jesus as He went about and ministered.

Is there a form of evangelism I do like? Well, as we work our way through the various forms of evangelism, I have frequently mentioned acts of love and service within interpersonal relationships. Some churches refer to this as "meeting needs." However, I am not a big fan of need-based evangelism either.

STOP MEETING NEEDS

For some reason, whenever some Christians start talking about the importance of just loving and serving people, there are others who get nervous. They say things like, "Oh, so you believe in a social gospel. You don't believe in in telling others the truth. You just want to ignore the issue of their sin and just meet their needs. That's not going to get anybody into heaven."

Please do not think I am advocating a social gospel. I am not. I do not think that the answer to aggressive, in-your-face evangelism strategies is to just shut up about the gospel and show people the gospel through our lives and actions instead. There are some churches who only try to love and serve people and never say anything whatsoever about God, sin, Jesus Christ, or eternal life. I think such churches have overcorrected and let the pendulum swing too far.

When it comes to need-based evangelism, we have two extremes.

---

[8] Gregory A. Boyd, *The Myth of a Christian Nation* (Grand Rapids: Zondervan, 2005), 158.

On the one side, we have churches that focus only on meeting people's physical needs. These are the social-gospel churches, which focus on need-based evangelism. They say things like, "People don't care how much you know until they know how much you care," or "An empty stomach has no ears." I have no argument with these proverbs. They are true. But I would add a proverb of my own: "Don't let busy hands tie your tongue." Sometimes these churches get so busy loving and helping people, they never get around to telling others the truth about God, sin, Jesus Christ, and eternal life.

The other church extreme criticizes the efforts of need-based evangelism as a waste of time and resources. "What good is it," they ask, "for people to go to hell with nice clothes and a full stomach?" They argue that a person's eternal destiny is more important than any earthly comfort. These churches say things like, "It's our job to preach; it's God's job to save," and "People are destroyed from lack of knowledge, not from lack of food" (alluding from Hosea 4:6). There is truth in these sayings as well.

But both sides, with their proverbs and passionate appeals, have missed the overarching message of the gospel, that it is good news for *both* the body *and* the spirit. For *both* temporal *and* eternal life. The gospel is not just about life here and now, nor is it about life in the hereafter. It is about both. The gospel is the full-orbed message about the claims of Jesus on both our present and eternal life. To focus on one life or the other is a serious mistake.

And yet among churches that focus on both the physical and spiritual elements of the gospel, there are still two subtle but serious mistakes that are often made. These two mistakes are only found in churches that are trying to meet both physical needs and spiritual needs, not just one or the other. In recent years, churches that try to meet both physical and spiritual needs have much more common than either of the extreme churches above. But they can still fall into one of two mistakes.

The first mistake is when we think that meeting a physical need is just preliminary to meeting the spiritual need. These churches believe that meeting the spiritual need is of primary importance, and meeting the spiritual need is simply a means to an end. Meeting physical needs is almost seen as a necessary evil. In this view, meeting physical needs is a waste of time and money unless they help the church accomplish its real goal of saving people's souls. In this view, meeting people's physical needs is not really part of the gospel, but is simply a way to gain a hearing for the gospel. For these churches, the gospel is still just a message about how to receive eternal life, and the free meals, the clothes closet, and community service projects are just ways of gathering an audience and grabbing people's ears.

Churches that function under this mindset usually require the people who show up to receive the free clothes, food, or counseling to sit through a gospel presentation as the "entrance fee." You want a free meal? Fine. First listen to this sermon. You want marriage counseling? Great. But let's first deal with your broken relationship with God. You want a free coat for the winter? We can give you one, but let me first go through this tract with you about how to get clothed with the righteousness of God. You want your car washed for free? We can do that. But while you wait, let me tell you how you can be washed from all your sin.

The problem with this is twofold. First, it cheapens the gospel. It makes us sound like we are selling timeshares in Florida: "You want a free vacation in the sunny Florida beaches? We'll give you one, but first you must sit through this high-pressure sales presentation." Is this really how we want to tell others about Jesus?

As with door-to-door evangelists and street-vendor-bullhorn preachers, any evangelistic approach which makes us look as if we are selling Jesus should be avoided at all costs. Jesus is not a commodity, and we are not salesmen.

The second mistake that churches make when they try to meet both the physical and spiritual needs of other people, and it is this: we can become so focused on the *needs* of people, that we neglect the people themselves. The needs become more important than the people. The need becomes a substitute for getting to know people who are dealing with those issues and needs. So sometimes, we need to forget the issues and forget the needs, and just focus on people. We need to stop categorizing and classifying people by their needs, and just love and serve them as people.

So forget all this talk about "people's greatest need is salvation, and so we meet that need by preaching the gospel." Far too often, Christians put off until eternity what should be done today. We see people in pain, suffering, and oppression crying out for help, and our normal response is, "Believe in Jesus for eternal life. Then, when you die, everything will be okay. God will wipe away your tears, right the wrongs, and judge those who are hurting you. Won't that be grand?"

Yet when they reject our gracious offer because we have nothing to offer them here and now for their suffering on earth, we consign them to eternal suffering in hell for their rejection of Jesus. When we refuse to help others with their physical needs because their greatest need is eternal life, the "Good News" message that many people hear is, "Your suffering in this life at the hands of wicked men will be followed by suffering in eternity at the hands of a loving God."

Is it any wonder that people reject the "Good News" when there seems to be nothing good about it?

This has happened to our gospel presentation because we have separated the gospel into two sides, the physical and the spiritual, and then set up the spiritual side as higher and more important than the physical. We do not realize it, but such thinking reveals that we have fallen into the trap of Gnostic dualism. Gnostic dualism is the idea that the universe is divided into two sides, the physical and the spiritual, and the physical side is mostly bad while the spiritual side is mostly good. Therefore, we should focus primarily on the spiritual side of life.

Dualism is so prevalent in churches today it is hard to recognize. But it is found in statements like, "Earth is not my home; I'm just passing through" and in the complacent and barely-masked glee that some churches feel when we hear about tsunamis, earthquakes, wars, disease, and famine destroying our world. "After all," we are told, "these are the signs that the end is near. The worse things get, the closer we are!" It is found in the idea of some churches that we can do whatever we want with our bodies and with this world, because the only thing that really matters is the condition of our soul. Dualism is found in the idea that we in the west are the enlightened ones, with our modern science and technology, and all the world must bow to our superior knowledge. It is found in the message of some sermons that seem to imply the belief that we can bomb people into freedom, justice, and liberty, that we can use and abuse this planet, because it will all burn in the end, and we're going to get a new earth anyway.

The basic problem with Gnostic dualism is that it severs people and issues into two. Dualistic thinking believes that people and issues have two sides: physical and spiritual, and the two never meet. Therefore, when we are meeting physical needs, it has nothing to do with spiritual needs, and meeting spiritual needs does nothing for the physical. But since the spiritual is clearly the more important of the two, if the physical needs are a necessary evil to gain access to the spiritual, then so be it.

It is far better to view people as both physical and spiritual, with both aspects being intimately connected and intertwined. There is no such thing as helping a person physically and not spiritually. Helping a person physically also helps them spiritually, and vice versa. Spiritual help pours over into all areas of life: emotional, mental, and physical. Churches must come to recognize that everything is spiritual, and everything is physical. The dividing line between the two where one is seen to be superior to the other, or one is seen as the doorway to the other is an artificial, unbiblical, and dangerous idea. The physical and spiritual were created together by God and must remain together. What God has joined together, let no man separate.

There is an account in the Gospel of Luke when Jesus encounters a man with a withered hand. Such a deformity would have kept this man from performing most kinds of work, and such a blemish may also have restricted his ability to bring sacrifices to God and participate with fellow Jews in the worship of God. This man was physically and spiritually outcast. Not only this, but the day on which Jesus met him was a Sabbath. So the situation is overflowing with numerous physical and spiritual needs, and complex theological issues.

But Jesus raised none of the issues, asked none of the theological questions, and focused on none of the needs. Jesus did not write a letter to the editor, make a plan to help others with similar problems, start a task force, raise support, begin a nonprofit organization to raise awareness for people with withered hands, address the cultural, sociological, and theological errors which had created the problem, or any of the other things He could have done. Instead, Jesus just helped the man. Jesus knew the man needed help and so Jesus helped him.

When a person with a need or issue is in front of us, our focus should be on that person, and not on the need or issue which that person represents. There will be plenty of time later to raise awareness for the plight of others facing the same need.

But the time for that is not when someone is standing right in front of us with that need. That is the time to toss all the plans, and fundraising, and support letters out the window, and just say, "Here, let me help." When we focus on helping people rather than "meeting needs," we view people as individuals with all the complex issues and histories and situations that comes with them. When dealing with individual people, we quickly realize there are no quick fixes or pat answers, and must commit to spending real time with real people for the long haul.

The problem with need-based evangelism is that it tends to focus on needs, rather than on people. Such an approach causes the ministries and ministry leaders to become self-centered. The ministry leaders want to find a "big need" so they can "make a splash" and "go big" in the community, in the hopes that the newspapers and news stations will notice, and give the church or ministry some free publicity. In this way, meeting a need of the community becomes about meeting our own need for recognition, honor, and glory. We must therefore be wary about doing our good deeds before men to be praised by them (cf. Matt 6:1-2).

But being "needs oriented" also causes people who have needs to become more self-centered. Learning about big needs in the community usually includes some sort of "Needs Survey." And when we go around asking people what their needs are, it trains them to think of God as someone who is just there to meet their needs. "Needs Surveys" train people to think only about themselves and ask, "How are you going to meet my needs?"

Ironically, if we were actually living among and with the people of the community, "Need Surveys" would be completely unnecessary. If we truly lived with and among the people we were trying to serve, we would already know what the needs are. Maybe we would be suffering and struggling with many of the same needs ourselves!

Worst yet, when we focus on meeting needs rather than just on loving people and living life with one another, while we may meet many needs in the community, we rarely get to know the actual people of the community. I remember building houses with Habitat for Humanity (a great community project!), but never actually meeting or learning the names of the people who we were building the house for! I remember having food drives and clothing drives in the churches I pastored, and when we delivered the food and clothes to needy family, we spent less than five minutes with each family because we had so many deliveries to make. We met needs, but never got to know any people.

Meeting needs is great, but loving people is better. Developing relationships one by one, and spending time talking with people takes more time and has small beginnings, but this is the way of the Kingdom of Heaven (Matt 13:31-32). Understanding the Kingdom of Heaven helps us better understand the message of the gospel and the goal of evangelism.

THE KINGDOM OF HEAVEN AND EVANGELISM

The Kingdom of Heaven is intimately tied with evangelism, but not in ways that most people believe. For many centuries now (at least since the Reformation and possibly before that) people have understood the "Kingdom of Heaven" (or the Kingdom of God) as being equivalent to "heaven." People have also noticed that in Scripture, the topics of the gospel and the Kingdom of Heaven are intimately connected. In many places in Scripture, the gospel *is* the message about the arrival of the Kingdom of Heaven.

So when people assume that the "Kingdom of Heaven" equals "heaven," and since a central message of the gospel is to invite people into the Kingdom of Heaven, then it seems logical to assume that the gospel message is focused on "How to get to heaven." It is for this reason that most evangelistic techniques and gospel presentations place a heavy emphasis on numbers of people who have "made decisions" for Christ. For many, evangelism is implicitly about how to achieve the maximum number of bodies we can usher into heaven before we go to heaven ourselves.

But in recent decades, many Christians around the world have begun to teach and write about the Kingdom of Heaven in a different way. They note, for example, that in Matthew 6:10 when Jesus prays about the Kingdom, it is not for people to enter into heaven, but for God's will to be done *on earth*, as God's will is already done *in heaven*. As a result of this and numerous other similar texts, many teachers and writers have argued that the Kingdom of Heaven is not heaven, but is rather God's rule and reign *on earth*. Praying that the Kingdom to be on earth as it is in heaven is to pray for the rule and reign of God on earth just as God rules and reigns in heaven.

With this understanding, we can see that the Kingdom of Heaven is already "in heaven," and through the life, death, and resurrection of Jesus, the Kingdom of Heaven is expanding to earth as well. It is not here fully, but the standard has been placed, and the claim has been made. The present rulers of this age are not happy with the arrival of the Rightful King, and so they fight with tooth and claw to hold on to their dominion, power, and authority. But we, as followers of Jesus, must continue the work He started in spreading the rule and reign of God across the entire earth and into the hearts and minds of every person. This good news is that God is restoring His rule and reign upon the earth, and this news is to be spread to all corners of the world, not just by what we say, but also by what we do. Our words proclaim the inauguration and arrival of the Kingdom of God, but our actions show that God is ruling and reigning in our own lives here and now. Our actions prove the reality of what we claim, that God is ruling and reigning in our own lives.

Therefore, the gospel message is about way more than just how to get to heaven when we die. Certainly, it includes truths about this, but the gospel is not just concerned with what happens after we die, but is even more concerned with what happens while we live. It is a message for the here and now; not just a message for the hereafter. It is a message about how the rule and reign of God has been planted in our own lives and is spreading and growing to cover every area of our life. It is a message about how through everything we say and do, seeds of the kingdom are being scattered into the lives of all people around us, with the hope that some of them may also come under the rule and reign of God. If all of this is true, what then does this mean for evangelism?

WHAT IS EVANGELISM?

If it is true that the gospel concerns all of life, so that living and proclaiming the gospel leads to the ever-increasing expansion of the rule and reign of God in our own lives, not just in what we say, but also in what we do and how we act, then what does this mean for evangelism?

To answer this question, it might be helpful to note that in Scripture, the words *evangelism* and *gospel* are essentially the same words. Frankly, I wish our Bible translators had shown this connection better, as it would have cleared up a lot of confusion about what the gospel is and how to do evangelism. Both words come from the Greek root *evangel*. As you can see, our word *evangelism* is not even a translation from the Greek! And as for the word "gospel," it is not the best translation either, but is a hybrid of Old English and German and means "good story" or "good message."

48

So the problem with translating the *evangel* word family is that there are not any good English words to translate it to. In the days of Jesus and the apostles, *evangel* referred to a good message which had immediate and lifelong positive implications for those who heard it. It was an announcement of liberty to the captives and freedom for the oppressed. It was the announcement that the enemy had been defeated, the war had been won. It was the declaration that the old ruthless and evil king had died, and a new king of peace, righteousness, and justice now sat on the throne. When someone heard these sorts of *evangel* messages, their lives would be forever different. The good message was so revolutionary that the simple act of telling it to others caused great joy and brought great freedom to all who heard it.

But the typical evangelistic message of today does no such thing. Why not? For two reasons. First, we are leaving out most of the message. The typical gospel presentation shares a few facts about a man named Jesus who lived 2000 years ago, and then a few facts about what happens to us after death as a result, but leaves out everything relating to our life here and now. As such, the gospel has been gutted of most of its persuasive power.

Secondly, even among those who do believe this pared-down gospel, there is no urgency to let the rule and reign of God expand in their lives, because this past and future gospel isn't concerned with the here and now. And when lives don't change, and people do not reflect the love and peace of Jesus Christ, then our gospel presentations lose even more power, because the people we are talking to do not see why any of it matters. When we are not changed by the gospel we preach, they are not persuaded to believe the gospel. If the gospel makes no difference to us, why should it make any difference to them whether they believe it or not?

So when we begin to understand that the gospel is about all of life, not just the past and the future, then we begin to view evangelism differently as well. When we remember that the words "gospel" and "evangelism" are based on the same words, and when we realize that the gospel is about all of life, then we begin to realize that evangelism is about all of life also. We begin to see that evangelism is not just something that takes place in a church with a preacher up front, or on a street corner when we pass out tracts, but is also something that takes place when we perform our jobs at work, when we fill out our taxes, buy groceries, and watch a football game with our neighbor. If the gospel is concerned with all of life, then the gospel affects how we act and behave in all of life's situations. Therefore, if the gospel is about all of life, then everything we do in life is, by definition, evangelistic.

This means something else as well. This means that evangelism is not a "one time event." Evangelism never stops. Just because someone "believes in Jesus" does not mean they have been "evangelized." Again, if the gospel is about how we live and act in all of life, then evangelism is also about how we live and act in all of life. Evangelism isn't over with someone just because they believe in Jesus. Before a person got to that point, evangelism had been going on for a very long time, and will continue to go on for the rest of that person's life.

In other words, you and I are not yet evangelized. Sure, we may believe truths about the gospel, and sure, we may have eternal life through believing in Jesus for it, but if the gospel is about all of life and seeing the rule and reign of God expand in our life, then we have not been fully evangelized until the rule and reign of God is complete in our lives. As this will never fully happen this side of eternity, we are "unevangelized."

Maybe some terminology changes would help make this clearer. No Christian would ever think that they have completed the path of discipleship. Following Jesus in discipleship is a lifelong process. And, by the way, discipleship begins before we ever believe in Jesus. A person can follow Jesus, listen to His teachings, and be drawn after Him long before they ever believe in Him for eternal life. So also, discipleship continues throughout the life of a believer. We are to forever be learning more about Jesus and seeking to love and serve others like Jesus. That is what discipleship is all about.

Think of evangelism the same way. If discipleship is a lifelong pursuit of the ways of Jesus, evangelism is a lifelong pursuit of the ways of the gospel, or the ways of the Kingdom of Heaven. Just as you never fully arrive in discipleship, but the process always continues, so also, you never fully arrive with evangelism, but the process of living the ways of the Kingdom continues throughout all of life. Just as discipleship begins before a person believes and continues throughout the entirety of the person's life, so also with evangelism. Evangelism, like discipleship, is a life-long process.

So do you want to do evangelism? Put down your bullhorn and your tracts. Forget what they taught you in your preaching course about the power of persuasive speech. Disregard all the tips and suggestions for engaging others in dialogue about the gospel. If you want to evangelize, all you need to do is learn to live the gospel in your everyday life. While this may include speaking words of truth to people you encounter on life's journey, it may also include taking plates of cookies over to your neighbors, mowing the lawn of the little old lady down the street, or being kind and generous to the lazy coworker at your job. All of these sorts of actions are based on Kingdom principles of loving God and loving your neighbor.

LOOK OUT!

So evangelism is not about telling people to look to heaven or to the afterlife as a cure for all of life's problems. Evangelism is not about getting more bodies into the pews at church or more souls through the gates of heaven. The central message of evangelism is not that we must "Get right with God because then eternity will be grand." Instead, while the gospel contains truth about heaven and eternity, the focus of the gospel is on life here on earth, seeking to bring all things under the rule and reign of God.

The gospel contains numerous truths about loving one another, taking care of our neighbor, looking after our family, and serving those in need. If we are ignoring these aspects of the gospel, we are not living or obeying the entire gospel, but are instead using the hope of heaven as a way to escape the responsibilities of life on earth. In his book *Naming the Powers*, Walter Wink put it this way:

> Christian evangelism has all too often been wedded to a politics of the status quo and merely serves to relieve stress by displacing hope to an afterlife and ignoring the causes of oppression.[9]

Rather than spending all our time singing songs, reading books, and gazing up into the sky waiting for Jesus to return in the clouds, we must begin looking out into the lives of the people around us, looking for ways to love, serve, and help them with their life here and now.

I am sure you have seen the bumper sticker which says, "Earth is not my home; I'm just passing through." Though it is true that we are "aliens and strangers" in this world (1 Pet 2:11), we must understand that the *reason* we are alive is not simply to wait for eternal life, but so that we can bless and help those around us get through this life. This is what the gospel is all about.

---

[9] Wink, *Naming the Powers*, 117.

Some central traits of the gospel-centered life are peace, mercy, justice, and compassion, all of which are not only to be practiced in eternity, but also right here, right now, on earth. So we must not sit idly around twiddling our thumbs while we wait for Jesus to return and set all things straight. We must anticipate His future rule and reign by trying to restore righteousness here and now. We look toward the future reign of God on earth by trying to live out the reign of God now. By living out the gospel in this way, we can pray with Jesus, "Thy kingdom come (now), thy will be done (now), on earth (now) as it is in heaven (now)."

So do you want to evangelize and share the gospel with others? Certainly, others must be told about what Jesus has done in the past, through His life, death, and resurrection, and how this affects our future in eternity. But we must also live out the truths of the gospel in our present, showing love, mercy, and grace to others, working to bring freedom to the oppressed, liberty to those in bondage, healing to the brokenhearted, and hope for those in despair. These are central truths of the gospel and why Jesus came (cf. Luke 4:17-21). As we follow Jesus in living the gospel, our evangelistic efforts will be more than words, and will include sacrificial acts of love and service.

The goal of the gospel and evangelism is not just getting butts into pews and bodies into heaven, but is about loving and serving others, right here, right now, on earth, in our lives. Until we learn to love and serve others, we have not begun to evangelize.

2

PASS ON THE OFFERING PLATE

*Is this the same preaching, when Christ says to
the rich young man, "Sell all that thou hast,
and give it to the poor;" and when the priest
says, "Sell all that thou hast and ... give it to
me"? —Søren Kierkegaard*

Several years ago, I visited a slum in Bangalore, India. After
walking through the slum and trying to serve some of the people that lived there, the team I was with happened upon a beautiful brick church building, complete with steeples and stained
glass. I was a little surprised to see such a building in the middle of such poverty and asked several of the people in the slum
about the church.

They had only good things to say about the church. The
church tried to offer food, clothing, and basic healthcare to the
people of the slum. Those who attended the church said that
they liked going. The music was beautiful. The pastor was
kind. And they said that the church was cool and clean, and
attending the church gave them some reprieve from the heat

and filth that surrounded them. Some said that the church gave them a glimpse of what heaven must be like. For them, it was a little bit of heaven on earth, a place to give them hope for the future in the midst of a life of hardship and despair.

Obviously, the people needed love and hope and this church was offering it to them. For that, I praise the church. Helping and serving the poor in such tangible ways should be a high priority for every church.

But as I talked with some of the people a bit more, I found out that almost all of them tithed to the church. And they were happy to do so. Not a single one complained about it. When I expressed surprise that they would give from their poverty, they reminded me of the story of the Widow's mite, in which the woman who gave her last two pennies was praised more by Jesus than those who gave from their wealth. They told me about the principle of tithing, that if we give to God generously and joyfully from what little we have, He would multiply what we gave, and give back to us from the overflowing storehouses of heaven. They told me that the first ten percent of what they earned went directly to God.

I went away amazed at their great faith.

But in later years, I began to wonder about the whole practice of tithes and offerings. I began to question the teaching of giving ten percent. I began to seriously study what the Bible teaches about the tithe.

And what I found shocked, surprised, and saddened me. As much good as that church did in the Bangalore slum, I now think it was a great sin to collect tithes from the people of the slum. It would have been much better for the church to *give* money to the poor people than to collect money from them, even if this meant firing some of their staff or selling their building.

In more recent years, I have discovered that having a lavish church building in the midst of poverty is not an isolated incident. It is not uncommon to go into some of the poorest and most destitute communities around the world where many of the people live in cardboard and tarpaper shacks and have barely enough food to live on, and in the middle of this community, find a large, grandly constructed church building with towering steeples, intricate stained glass, beautiful woodwork, and gorgeous hand-painted murals. More often than not, the priests and pastors of these churches are living quite comfortably as well.

In 2001 I went with a mission's trip to Kino, Mexico, a poor fishing village on the shore of the Gulf of California. Many of the families of this village lived in tarpaper shacks and slept on a dirt floor. Yet right in the middle of town was a large, brick church building, complete with stained glass and steeples. I don't know the story of how it was built, where the money came from, who was hired to construct it, or anything about the building, but I still remember thinking that the people of the community might have been better served if that church building never existed.

It is not always true that fancy churches are found in poverty stricken areas. Frequently the churches in poor neighborhoods have ramshackle and dilapidated buildings just like every other building in the area. And my goal in this chapter is not to criticize church buildings. As will be seen in the next chapter, church buildings are like anything else: they can be used for good purposes—to love and serve others—or they can be used for evil purposes—to give power, fame, and glory to individuals and organizations which are greedy for money and want to control others.

My main concern in this chapter is discuss the symbol that fancy church buildings represent. Despite the painted murals, the stained-glass window, the steeple pointing to heaven, and the 30-foot, spotlight-illuminated cross near the parking lot, church buildings do not represent Jesus as much as they represent money. This chapter will take a look at another of the three things that people associate with church: money.

A CHURCH MADE OF MONEY

Bodies, bucks, and bricks are the three pillars of the modern method of doing church. Church attendance, church tithing, and church buildings seem to be what concerns most churches. In some churches, there is little else preached on during the year except being more faithful and active members of the church, being more faithful in giving of money to the church, and helping the church expand its building or pay off its mortgage debt. Of these, money is often the biggest topic. Money is what makes the church world go round.

While the Bible does contain many texts on the topic of money, the emphasis that the church seems to place on money causes some to wonder if money has taken precedent over the concerns of the Kingdom, so that we have fallen prey to the siren call of mammon. Jacques Ellul writes about it this way:

> Grace has been put on sale, or the church has become a center of rapine and self-enrichment, or it is so obsessed with its financial problems that all its other concerns and functions take second place. In a hundred ways money has effectively corrupted the church. But what we see here is not just the world of money itself or our subjective desire for it. It is in truth a demonic power that has given money the ability to change everything that ought to be free and open grace into bitter conquest, possession, and obsession.[10]

---

[10] Jacques Ellul, *The Subversion of Christianity* (Grand Rapids: Eerdmans, 1986), 177-178.

This mammon worship is easily concealed under the guise of a spiritual practice called "tithing." We have fallen to the temptation of the devil and his offer of the riches of this world.

The goal of this chapter is to question to the practice of collecting tithes and offerings. We will look at the history of tithing, the Scriptural passages used to defend it, and some alternative solutions for how churches and ministries can raise money for their ministry needs.

THE HISTORY OF TITHING

The practice of tithing, as it is taught today in many churches, is only about 300 years old. It did not exist in the days of Jesus. It was not taught or practiced in the churches planted by Paul. Even where we do read in Scripture about tithing (a few places in the Old Testament, and fewer still in the New), the practice then was not at all what we are encouraged to practice today. The practice of giving 10% of your income to the church is a completely modern invention.

In the next section, we will look at some of the Scriptural passages used to defend the practice of tithing, but for now, we must understand how the teaching on tithing became common in the church.

Roughly the first 1000 years of the church operated under the Client-Patron system. Under this system, wealthy patrons would offer to protect, sponsor, and provide for the needs of others in exchange for work and service. Wealthy patrons would often provide for the needs of scholars, philosophers, and doctors in exchange for their full-time service. So if you wanted to be a philosopher, doctor, or religious teacher, you had two choices. You either had to pay your own way by having a job, or you had to find a patron who would take you on as a client and pay your way for you.

We see examples of both in Scripture. Jesus was trained as a carpenter, but He did not support His ministry through carpentry. Instead, it appears that He had a small network of patrons who supported His work and ministry. Luke 8:3 indicates that Jesus had several followers who provided for Jesus out of their wealth. In others words, Jesus was their client. They believed in what He was doing, and so they supported Him so He could do it full time.

It appears that others in the New Testament were similarly supported. It is likely that Luke, as a physician and historian, was the client of Theophilus (Luke 1:1-4, Acts 1:1). John encourages some of his readers to support the work of certain men, because in so doing, they would have a share in their work (3 John 7-8).

But this was not the only way of doing ministry. Paul is the best-known example of the other way. He supported himself by making tents. He had a trade which could travel with him, and it appears that whenever he ran out of money, he would go work for a local tentmaker to join in their work, and so receive payment (Acts 18:3). He did not ask for money from others to support his work, but supported himself by working (Acts 20:33-34; 2 Cor 11:9; 2 Thess 3:8-10).

Outside of the New Testament, we see these two methods referenced over and over in the writings of the early church fathers. Some worked with their hands and supported themselves. Others sought out a patron to provide for their needs and give them food and clothes so they could teach, travel, study, and write. Typically, the first few lines of a book indicate whether an early church father was a client or not, as those who have patrons usually always dedicate their book or pamphlet to their patron. For example, the patron of St. Jerome was Pope Damasus, and Jerome makes frequent references to works that had been commissioned to him by Damasus, and that once written, they would be dedicated to Damasus.

The fact that the Pope was a patron raises an interesting point. At this stage in church history, the spiritual leader in the church of Rome was also a client. The elder of the church in Rome was a client of the Roman Empire. When Emperor Constantine converted to Christianity and made it the official religion of the Roman Empire, the church was unified with the Roman Empire, and was viewed as a client to the Empire. The Empire turned over all the pagan temples and most of the pagan priests to the church, and paid for them all out of the Empires vast tax and war revenue. So all of the church buildings were owned and paid for by the Empire, and many of the clergy members also received their income from the government.

Once the Roman Empire became "Christian" most of the wealthy ruling class wanted to remain on good terms with the Emperor, and so most converted to Christianity. Many of these took the Christian message seriously and began to give from their wealth to the poor, the sick, the widows, and the orphans. Frequently, the church leaders were the ones who knew where the greatest needs existed, and sometimes the wealthy would simply give their money to the church so that the church could disperse it for the greatest good. Through this process, the church became increasingly wealthy, and over time, became a central power structure in the world.[11] In this way, the church functioned as both a client and a patron. It was a client to the Roman Empire (or the Emperor) and provided services to help maintain the peace and provide legitimacy to the decisions and rulings of the Emperor in exchanges for protection, tax revenue, and political power. But the church was also a patron. It used its power, revenue, and position to support great works of art, science, and literature, as well as to provide income to a vast number of priests, artists, doctors, scholars, and theologians so that their works would further benefit the power and position of the church.

---

[11] Ibid., 31.

For the most part, this is the way churches and clergy were supported for the next 1000 to 1500 years. Through a series of political maneuvers and power struggles, the Catholic Church and the Roman Empire melded together, but the Client-Patron system functioned in various ways and forms. This sort of system still lingers on in certain European countries that have state-funded churches. Even here in the United States, we are "clients" to the government in the sense that we have "tax exempt" status, but only if we refrain from endorsing candidates or speaking out against out patron government. If we do these things, our patrons may fine us or take away our tax-exempt status. (This might not be such a bad thing, but we'll discuss that idea later in this chapter.)

So although remnants of the Client-Patron system still exist today, something happened about 1000 years ago which caused the church to look for new forms of revenue and income. It was this event that also caused the church to begin consistently preaching and teaching about the necessity and importance of the "tithe."

Up until the late eighth century AD, the church buildings and most of the clergy were funded by the national and local governments. The expense was enormous and so some local governments began to excise additional taxes on the people, which went to help cover the costs of maintaining the church buildings and clergy. In seeking justification for this "religious tax" local governments turned to the Mosaic Law. The explanation given to the people by the church and government authorities was that God instituted a 10% tax on the people of Israel to support the Levitical Priesthood and the construction of the tabernacle and temple. This is not exactly true (as we will see below), but it is the explanation that was given when the government added a 10% tax on people to cover the costs of local church buildings and clergy.

However, this practice of enforcing a religious tax on the populace was not in widespread use until the late eighth century AD, when Emperor Charlemagne developed the parish system for the church. He wanted to control what the churches were teaching, and who got selected as bishops and priests in a particular church. So with the help of various church leaders, he developed the parish system. This system also required an exponential increase in the number of archbishops in the church so that they could oversee these newly founded parishes. The archbishops, in coordination with the local civic rulers, were given the responsibility of hiring and paying clergy to oversee all the people in a particular parish. To cover the expenses of these archbishops and the related bureaucracy, Emperor Charlemagne instituted a 10% mandatory tax on all the people in the parish. Once again, the archbishops, priests, and political rulers based this tax off of the Mosaic principle of the 10% tithe.[12]

People still gave additional funds when they attended church on Sunday or for a weekday Mass, but these were not considered part of the "tithe." People gave these funds as they always had, simply to support the ministry of their church, or to provide funding for additional services, such as baptisms, marriages, funerals, a personal Mass from the Priest, extra prayers said by a Monk, or even the forgiveness of sins. None of this giving was mandatory, of course.

Around 1200 AD, the tax burden on the poor had become so high, many of them cried out to their local priests and ruling authorities for relief. The vast majority of the clergy and civic leaders had become quite wealthy from the tax system, and simply ignored the pleas. But some listened and approached

---

[12] See Kenneth Scott Latourette, *The History of Christianity*, 2 vols. (Peabody, MA: Prince, 2005), 355-357, 526; Diarmaid MacCulloch, *Christianity: The First Three Thousand Years* (New York: Viking, 2009), 368-369.

Pope Innocent III in Rome for a tax relief from the 10% mandatory church tax, also known as the "tithe." In response, Pope Innocent III ordered that tithes for the support of the church be given precedence over all other taxes.[13] In other words, the Pope wanted taxes to be cut, but the 10% tax for the church should not be cut. If civic and religious leaders wanted to reduce the tax burden on the people in their parish, they should do so by cutting taxes *other* than the 10% church tax. Needless to say, very little tax cutting occurred.

This situation of viewing the "tithe" as a mandatory tax on all citizens of a particular parish continued until about 300 years ago, until the development of the novel idea about the separation of church and state. Once the church divorced herself from the oversight and control of the local and national governments, the church also no longer had the significant source of tax income which the government had previously collected on behalf of the church. But this was no problem, for the principle of the tithe was already firmly planted in the minds, theology, and practice of most people. Rather than funneling this 10% tax through the government, the church now became the direct recipient. The church continued to teach the people that the principle of the tithe still stood, but that now, rather than send this money to the church through the government tax collectors, the people could give it directly to the church itself.

To encourage and enforce this practice, all the same Scriptures and arguments were used. Though it was no longer thought of as a "tax" the church continued to teach that a tenth (or "tithe") of a person's income should go the church. They taught that this 10% tithe was instituted by God through Abraham and Moses, and was supported by the Prophets, Jesus, and the Apostles. The church taught that the purpose of this "tithe" was to maintain the church property and buildings, support the

---

[13] Latourette, *The History of Christianity*, 484.

church priesthood and clergy, and help cover the costs of the church ministry and programs.

And that brings us to where we are today. Messages about Abraham's tithe to Melchizedek, and the Mosaic law of giving 10% are frequently heard from pulpits around the world. Christians of all types are encouraged to "give to Caesar what is Caesar's and give to God what is God's," to be like the widow who gave her last two pennies and so received the praise of Jesus, and to follow the instructions of Paul to give generously and joyfully for the ministry of the church.

Most people never question such teaching. We assume it is correct. We believe what we have been told: that money is the root of all evil, that we cannot love both God and mammon, and that best way to defeat the love of money is to give it away. We never question such teachings. We never even bother to look them up in Scripture.

If we did, we might be surprised at what Scripture actually teaches about tithing.

THE TRUTH ABOUT TITHING

Though there are numerous Scripture passages about tithing, there are not as many as people think. While money is one of the most written-about subjects in the Bible, texts about tithing are relatively rare. Only eleven books in the Bible mention tithing, and of these, only one biblical author wrote actual commands about the practice. The biblical passages that refer to tithing are these: Genesis 14:20; Leviticus 27:30-32; Numbers 18:24-28; Deuteronomy 12:6-17; 14:22-28; 26:12; 2 Chronicles 31:5-12; Nehemiah 10:37-38; 12:44; 13:5-12; Amos 4:4; Malachi 3:8-10; Matthew 23:23; Luke 11:42; 18:12; and Hebrews 7:5-9.

We will look at most of these passages below, as well as several texts which many people use to defend the practice of tithing, such as the poor widow who gave her last two coins, and the instruction from Paul in 2 Corinthians 8–9 about generous and joyful giving. By looking at these passages, we will see that while giving from our income is praised and recommended, tithing is not a command that people must follow today, and even where tithing was commanded in biblical history, there were detailed and surprising instructions on what was to be done with the tithe.

Let us begin by looking at the first time tithing is mentioned in Scripture: the time when Abraham tithed to Melchizedek, the King-Priest of Salem.

The Tithe of Abraham. One of the most famous passages in Scripture about tithing is Genesis 14:18-20. In this passage, Abraham's nephew Lot has been taken captive by an invading army. Abraham gathers his trained men and pursues this army to rescue Lot. Abraham is successful, and returns from the battle with Lot, Lot's family, all the people who had also been taken captive, and all the goods and possessions which had been carried away. On their return trip, Melchizedek, the King-Priest of Salem, comes out to meet them and he blesses Abraham and blesses God. In response, Abraham gave to Melchizedek a tenth (or a tithe) of all the plunder from the battle. That is everything that this text says about tithing. One little line.

This passage would probably not be so prominent in the tithing debate if it were not for the comments on this passage by the author of the book of Hebrews. In Hebrews 7, the author of Hebrews makes the claim that Jesus is superior to the Levitical Priesthood. He begins this argument in 7:1-10 with a rather complex discussion about who has the right to receive tithes, and that Melchizedek is superior to the Levitical priests because through "the loins" of Abraham, the Levites paid a tithe to Melchizedek. Frankly, the whole argument sounds somewhat silly to modern ears, but was quite consistent with Hebraic ways of thinking about their ancestors and helps solve the dilemma about how Jesus could be our High Priest even though He was not of the Tribe of Levi.

Ultimately, however, Hebrews 7 is not at all about tithing, but is about Jesus being a superior High Priest. Nevertheless, this text is often brought up in connection with Genesis 14:18-20 to defend the practice of tithing in churches today. It is argued that since Abraham gave a tenth of his income to Melchizedek, and that since Melchizidek is a "type" of Jesus, then Abraham, and all descendants of Abraham, whether physical descendants by blood or spiritual descendants by faith, must also tithe to Jesus. A pastor who teaches the passage this way will argue that we give our tithe to Jesus by giving it to Jesus' priestly representative, which in our day is the pastor or priest of the church.

But notice that this is not at all what either Genesis 14 or Hebrews 7 are saying or teaching.

First, nowhere in either text is there a command for subsequent generations to follow the example of Abraham. In both Scriptures, Abraham's tithe to Melchizedek is described, but not prescribed. We are told what Abraham did, but we are not told that all people must do the same thing. If we are going to read a law or command into this text, we must invent it.

But secondly, we have even missed what the text says about Abraham's tithe. Genesis 14 implies what Hebrews 7 makes explicitly clear: Abraham gave a tenth of the spoils of war to Melchizedek. This was not a tenth of Abraham's possessions, nor was it a tenth of Abraham's annual income, nor was it even a regular offering which Abraham made to the local priest. This was a one-time gift from possessions which Abraham had just captured in war, the remainder of which, he returned to their original owners, the kings and people of Sodom and Gomorrah. Technically, Abraham gave 10% to the King-Priest of Salem, and 90% to the King of Sodom. He did allow his own soldiers to take a portion as well for payment, but we are not told how much (Gen 14:24). There is no instruction, command, or requirement here given to all people of all time about the necessity to give 10% of their income to God, to a minister, or to a church. Even for Abraham, this was only a one-time gift of possessions he had captured in war.

So *if* we were going to follow the true example of Abraham in Genesis 14 for a practice of tithing, the only time we would have to tithe to a local church was when we gained some possessions that were not ours, and before returning these possessions to their rightful owner, we gave 10% to the church. And remember, in Abraham's case, the rightful owner was the King of Sodom, who was probably not the most righteous man in the area (see Genesis 18–19).

There is one other example in Scripture of a portion of plunder being given to priests after a war. This second event is in Numbers 31:25-30. The Israelites went and attacked the Midianites and captured all their possessions. Upon their victorious return, God told Moses to tell the Israelites to divide the spoils into two parts: half should go to the soldiers who went out to battle, and the other half should go to everyone else. But after they divide the spoils for distribution, everybody was required to give a portion to God by giving it to the priests. And how much were they to give? The soldiers were to give $1/500^{th}$ and everybody else was to give $1/50^{th}$. Altogether, the total "tithe" given to the priests in this case comes to 1.1%.

It is extremely interesting that while these two passages are nearly identical in content and message (people go off to war, win plunder, and give a portion to the priest), the passage where *one person* gives 10% of the plunder to *a foreign priest* is a popular passage on tithing, while the passage where *all the people* of Israel give only 1.1% of the plunder to *their very own priests* is never preached on in sermon series about tithing. Yet when it comes to a passage about God commanding all people to give a certain portion of money to their own priests, the second passage is much clearer. Yet because the portion of money is only 1.1% instead of 10%, I doubt you will ever hear this second passage preached on as an example of how much of your money you should give to the church.

In both passages, however, there are no instructions or commands for God's people, either then or now, to give a portion of their *regular, annual income* to God by giving it to the priests. Both are simply examples of gifts that were given to priests from the plunder that was taken in war. In neither case is anyone consistently tithing of their annual income to support the work of God. Therefore, neither passage can be used to support the modern practice of tithing.

The Law of Moses. Moses is the only biblical author to write any commands about the tithe. Yes, that is right. There are no commands written by any other author in all of Scripture about giving a tenth of your income.

Even then, some pastors rightly point out that Moses' instructions about tithing were not for a mere 10%, but were closer to 30% of a person's annual income.

The argument for this 30% tithe is based on several passages from the Books of Moses. There was a tithe to support the Levites (Lev 27:30-33), a tithe to fund an annual festival (Deut 14:22-29), several smaller tithes to help the poor (Lev 19:9-10), a reduction in income to give rest to the land (Exod 23:10-11), and on top of all of this, there were numerous annual sacrifices of bulls and goats, all of which cost money (Lev 1-7). None of this counted the additional freewill offerings a person might make. Not counting the freewill offerings, then, it is estimated that a person's annual required "tithe" to the temple was not 10%, but was closer to 30% of their annual income.

You will occasionally hear pastors preach this, but usually it is just as a way of saying, "Thank God you don't have to give 30%! The normal 10% will be just fine." Though actually, such sermons usually begin with the biblical truth that in reality,

100% of what we have belongs to God. So the sermon structure follows this pattern: "100% belongs to God; the Israelites only had to give 30%; but we today only need to give 10%."

People who argue this, however, fail to recognize that when Moses wrote these laws, they were operating as a Theocracy, and the vast majority of these "tithes" were the modern equivalent of taxes. When the people brought in the required tithes of their crops and produce, it was so the rulers of the country could perform their God-given functions. And who were the rulers of the country in the Israelite theocracy set up by the Mosaic Law? The Levitical priests!

So while it is true that the Israelites gave somewhere in the vicinity of 30% of their crops and herds to support the work of the Levites, this is not at all equivalent to tithing to support the church today. Instead, since their "tithe" was supporting their theocratic government, the modern equivalent to the theocratic tithe is how we pay taxes to support the functions of our own democratic government (here in the United States, anyway). And when we realize that the average person today is paying the federal government around 25% of their income, and then paying another 10% (or more) for state, county, and city taxes, we are already paying a little more in taxes today than what was prescribed by the Mosaic Law for the people of Israel to support the functions of their government. To ask people to "tithe" an additional 10% to the church because "this is what the Law says" reveals a deep misunderstanding of the Mosaic Law, how this tithe was collected, and what this income was used for.

Let us look at the passages from the Mosaic Law in more detail, to see what they really say. When people teach about the law of the tithe, they usually go to a few passages in the Mosaic Law.

One of the most popular Scripture passages on tithing is Deuteronomy 14:22. It says this: "You shall truly tithe all the increase of your grain that the field produces year by year." A similarly popular passage is Leviticus 27:30: "And all the tithe of the land, whether of the seed of the land or of the fruit of the tree, is the Lord's. It is holy to the Lord." These passages are often used to defend the practice of reserving 10% of a person's income for God because these passages indicate that the tithe belongs to God; it does not belong to us.

What does the Mosaic Law say should be done with the tithe? It says the tithe belongs to God, but if so, how can a person give it to God? Again, modern pastors and Bible teachers who defend the practice of tithing will often turn to another passage in the writings of Moses to explain what should be done with the tithe. Numbers 18:24 says this: "For the tithes of the children of Israel, which they offer up as a heave offering to the Lord, I have given to the Levites as an inheritance." Since the modern equivalent of a Levitical priest is a pastor, it is often argued that the tithes should go to support the work of the pastor, or at least the ministry of the church.

And this is pretty much how it works. People give a portion of their income to the church, and about one-half of this money goes to pay the pastor's salary, and the other half goes to pay for the church building and programs.

But is this actually what the Mosaic Law teaches? Not quite. If we carefully examine these passages in context, a different picture emerges about what these tithes are for. For example, although Deuteronomy 14:22 is a popular verse on tithing, the following verses say what this tithe is to be used for. Notice the shocking instructions in Deuteronomy 14:23 and 26 about what to do with the tithe:

> And you shall eat before the Lord your God, in the place where He chooses to make His name abide, the tithe of your grain and your new wine and your oil, of the firstborn of your herds and your flocks, that you may learn to fear the Lord your God always....

71

And you shall spend that money for whatever your heart desires: for oxen or sheep, for wine or similar drink, for whatever your heart desires; you shall eat there before the Lord your God, and you shall rejoice, you and your household.

Wait! What? The tithe from the people is for them to spend on themselves? For whatever their heart desires? For food and drink?

Yes. That's right. The tithe of Deuteronomy 14 was intended to be spent on a big family feast. The text states that they should bring a tenth of their crops and a tenth from the newborn of their herds, and come together with everybody else, and have a big party. They will kill the oxen and sheep, and then cook and eat it. They shall take the grain and oil, and bake bread. They shall take the grapes and make wine. If there is money, they should use it buy whatever their heart desires. And when everybody has come together, they throw big, giant party! At this party, they are to eat, enjoy life, feast, drink, laugh, sing, and dance!

What about giving to the Levitical Priests? Well, they also were invited to join the party and eat and drink as much as they wanted (Deut 14:27). But the tithe was not for them, but for the families who brought them, to celebrate and enjoy life together with God.

This is what they were supposed to do once every two years. For two years, the entire tithe went for these communal family celebrations. On the third year, however, things changed. On the third year, the people of Israel were supposed to forego the celebration, and on this year, give the total tithe of crops and animals to the Levitical priests, and to the poor, the orphans, and the widows in the community (Deut 14:28-29; 26:12-14). So it is true that a tithe was paid to the Levitical priests. But this tithe was only once every three years, and it was also to be distributed to the poor and needy in the community. It was not for the priests only.

Furthermore, this tithe paid to the Levitical priests and the community poor was not a tithe from the total number of the flock and herd, nor was it even ten percent of the total number of newborns. Instead, according to Deuteronomy 12:17, it was only a tenth of the *firstborn* from the flock. Every female animal only has one firstborn. After that, no other calf or lamb was a firstborn. So this 10% tithe was only of the firstborn animals of the flock. Furthermore, it was not even the *best* 10% of the firstborn, but, according to Leviticus 27:32-33, the 10% from the firstborn of the flock was to be *randomly chosen*. To randomly choose the tithe from the firstborn of the flock, they would line up all the firstborn animals, and drive them past a Levite who would select every tenth animal with a rod.

All of this paints a radically different picture about tithing than we are ever taught in church. First of all, this 10% tithe only goes to the priests every third year. During the first and second years, the tithe was still collected, but it was to be spent by the family itself for a big family celebration. Secondly, in the third year, when the tithe was given to the Levites, the tithe from the animals was not 10% of their total possessions, nor even 10% of their total income (all newborn animals), but was 10% of the firstborn animals only, and this 10% was not the best of the flock, but was randomly chosen. Finally, this tithe from the third year did not go to the Levites only, or even for the needs of the tabernacle, but was to be shared with anyone in the community who had need. The poor, the orphans, and the widows were specifically mentioned as deserving of care.

It appears then that there is no basis in the Mosaic Law for the practice of tithing 10% of our total annual income to the local church. The only commands about tithing in Scripture are for the people of Israel living in a theocracy, and they are to tithe 10% to their own family for two years, and then in the third year, give 10% to the Levitical Priests and the poor in the community.

If we truly wanted to draw some principles from the Mosaic Law for our practice today, we could say that families should put aside a portion of their income every year to enjoy life by participating in special festivals and feasts with their family. Every third year, some funds can also go to support a ministry of our choosing, and for taking care of the poor, the orphans, and the widows in our community.

If we were going to try to follow closely the Mosaic Law about tithing, a family's budget might look like this:

Year 1: 10% for Family Celebration
Year 2: 10% for Family Celebration
Year 3: 10% for Ministry Support and Loving Others

Technically, they went through this cycle twice, and then in the seventh year, gave the land a "rest" so that there was no planting or harvesting, and therefore, no tithing from the crops. I doubt that anyone today is able to take every seventh year off from work, but that also was part of the cycle of God's economy for Israel. On top of this, every fiftieth year was to be reserved for a huge, national, year-long party, during which time all debts would be cancelled, all slaves set free, and all land would revert to the original owner. But again, I doubt most people would be able to practice this part of God's economic plan today. Once again, this shows how selective our churches are today in picking and choosing which parts of God's economic plan we want to enforce.

Yet while I would never command Christian families to follow certain elements of the Mosaic Law, I do believe that the three-year cycle of tithing is something that many families could implement with great success. Imagine the party you could have with your family if you put aside 10% of your money every month and saved it up for one big giant bash every year! This is not selfish living; this is joyful living in God's good creation. Not only that, most families could use such annual celebrations with each other. Such celebrations would strengthen the family bond, create memories of joy and laughter, and help each other focus on the goodness and greatness of God in their lives during the previous year.

And of course, every third year, the annual celebration money would not go for a family party, but for helping a local ministry and providing for the needs of the poor in the community.

Let me offer a word of caution, however. I am not recommending an additional 10% over what you are *already* spending on vacations and entertainment. In modern Western civilization, we suffer from something which almost nobody else in the history of the world has suffered from: materialistic abundance. The reason for the 10% tithe for a family celebration in biblical times is because families didn't normally have the time or the money to do such things. Living in an agrarian society, most Israelites worked 12 hour days from sun-up to sun-down, six days a week (72 hours per week), taking only the Sabbath (Saturday) off as a day of rest. All this work barely provided enough food to feed the family. So saving 10% of their income for a special family celebration was something unique and exciting.

Today, however, most of us work much less than 72 hours per week, and spend much more than 10% a year on fun, feasting, and family activities. We go out to eat in restaurants and gorge ourselves on a weekly basis. We take family trips a few times a year. I would not be too surprised if some families are spending way more than 10% of their annual income on feasting and family celebrations. If you take everything you spend on eating out, going to movies, taking trips, and "enjoying life" and it comes to more than 10% of your annual income, you don't need to spend an additional 10% so that you can feast more often, and go on more trips. Instead, you might actually want to cut back on the amount of money you are "tithing" to your family, and spend more money on loving and serving others, helping the poor, taking care of orphans and widows, and showing the love of Jesus to others. This truly is the tithe that matters to God (cf. Isa 58:6-9). And in fact, when we get into the instructions in the New Testament and from Jesus about what to do with our money, we will see that the money principles of the Kingdom of God place a heavy emphasis on providing for others in need.

But before we get to the teaching of Jesus and the apostles about how to use our money, let us turn to one final passage in the Hebrew Scriptures about tithing: Malachi 3:8-10.

Stealing from God. Malachi 3:8-10 is by far the most preached-upon passage on tithing in the entire Bible. It is a popular passage because it seems to announce a curse upon those who fail to tithe to God. Using this passage, pastors and preachers tell people that if they want to be blessed financially, they must bring in the full tithe. If they fail in this, they are robbing God and will be cursed. Sounds ominous, right?

The text says this:

Will a man rob God?
Yet you have robbed me.
But you say,
"In what way have we robbed You?"
In tithes and offerings.

You are cursed with a curse,
For you have robbed Me,
Even the whole nation.

Bring all the tithes into the storehouse,
That there may be food in My house.

And try Me now in this,
Says the Lord of hosts,
If I will not open for you the windows of heaven
And pour out for you such blessing
That there will not be room enough to receive it.

It seems pretty clear. If we do not tithe the full amount we are supposed to, we are robbing God and will be cursed. But if we bring the full tithe, then God will make us rich, so rich, we cannot even hold it all. The pastor who preaches on this text admonishes the people to give their full tithe to the church, and bring their full offerings so that they can be blessed by God rather than cursed.

Yet this is simply another passage that has been severely misunderstood and misapplied because people fail to understand the historical background of Malachi. To understand what this passage is saying, we must begin by looking at the historical context.

In 538 BC, a man named Zerubbabel was given permission by Cyrus, the king of Persia, to return to Israel and rebuild the temple in Jerusalem (Ezra 1–2). The process of rebuilding the temple experienced many setbacks and difficulties, so the prophets Haggai and Zechariah encouraged the people to continue rebuilding the temple despite all of the problems. Finally, after over 20 years, the temple was completed in 515 BC (Ezra 6). Nevertheless, a completed temple did not restore Israel's obedience to God's law. The priesthood was corrupt and the people were intermarrying with pagans, so in 458 BC, Ezra traveled to Jerusalem and worked to correct these moral failures (Ezra 9–10).

Fourteen years later, Nehemiah also travelled to Jerusalem, this time with the goal of rebuilding the walls of Jerusalem. Along with rebuilding the walls, he was also able to enact many reforms to the way people live and worship. It was during this time of reforms under Nehemiah that Malachi lived and taught. Some of the issues that Malachi addressed in his teaching were the same issues that Nehemiah addressed. One of these issues is bringing the tithes and offerings into the storehouse of the temple for the rebuilding efforts.

In the historical record of Nehemiah, it appears that the people of Israel loved to have priests and Levites ministering in the temple, and were thrilled to give of their tithes and offerings to support this ministry. It was what God commanded, and they rejoiced in giving of their crops and herds (Neh 12:44). Nehemiah specifically says that in his days, all Israel joyfully participated in giving the portions required by the law (Neh 12:47). So far, this does not sound at all like the issue Malachi is concerned with. The people were giving joyfully and generously to the temple reconstruction efforts and the ministry of the priests and Levites.

Yet in Nehemiah 13, we read of a priest named Eliashib who had been given the authority over the storehouse in the Temple (13:4). It was his job to make sure that all the singers, gatekeepers, priests, and Levites who served in the Temple received their portion of the grain, wine, and oil that had been brought by the people of Israel (13:5). But he was doing no such thing. Instead, he had removed all of the grain, wine, and oil, and had allowed a man named Tobiah to begin living in the storehouse instead (13:4, 7). And who was Tobiah? He was the enemy of Israel who had tried to stop the people from rebuilding the wall (Neh 2:10-19; 6:10-19)! As a result, the Levites and the temple singers were not getting their daily portions of food, and so rather than serve in the temple, they had been forced to go back to their fields so that they could feed themselves and their families (Neh 13:10).

What was Eliashib doing with the grain, the wine, and the oil that had been stored in the storehouse, and which the Israelites continued to give? The text does not say exactly, but after Nehemiah kicks Tobiah out of the storehouse, he brought the *grain* back into the storehouse, but the text says nothing about the wine and oil. A few verses later, Nehemiah calls on the people of Israel to replenish the storehouses with grain, wine, and oil (cf. Neh 13:9, 12), and Nehemiah appointed new treasurers over the storehouse who would properly and fairly distribute the portions to the temple workers (Neh 13:13).

With this background in mind, we can now return to Malachi. But before we jump to Malachi 3, let us look at the context of the book itself, to see if there are any further hints about the message of Malachi. When studying a book of the Bible, one of the primary things to look for is who the book is addressed to. That is, who is written to? Who is the audience? Who did the author have in mind when he wrote? With Malachi, this question is easily answered, for Malachi refers to them directly several times. In several places, Malachi reveals that he is addressing the priests of Israel (1:6; 2:1), and the sons of Levi (3:3).

If the book of Malachi is directed primarily to certain priests and Levites, then what is it these priests are doing? Malachi tells us this as well. They sneer at the commands of God, saying such things are "weariness" (1:13). They bring contemptible offerings to God, animals that are stolen, sick, and lame (1:13). They exploit wage earners, widows, and orphans (3:5). And they are robbing God of the tithes and offerings that belong to Him (3:8-10).

Based on such contextual issues, it appears that the section on tithing in Malachi 3:8-10 is not so much addressed to the people of Israel, who apparently were doing a good job of bringing their tithes and offerings to the storehouse, but to the wicked and wayward priests, and specifically Eliashib, who were removing the tithes and offerings from the storehouse for their own personal gain. Though the text does not say what they were doing with the tithes and offerings of grain, wine, and oil, it seems likely they were either hoarding these items for themselves, or were selling them for personal profit.

That these verses are speaking specifically to the priests is clear from the little phrase at the end of Malachi 3:9. God says that they are not only robbing God, but are robbing the entire nation as well. This statement does not make much sense if the people are failing to bring the tithes and offerings into the storehouse. But if the people *are* bringing in the tithes and offerings (as Nehemiah indicates that they were), but the priest was stealing them for himself and his friends, then it is easy to see how they were stealing from God *and* from the nation as well.

So in taking Nehemiah 13 and Malachi 3 together, it appears that the people of Israel had brought tithes and offerings into storehouse, but Eliashib had stolen and squandered them. At Nehemiah's request, the people of Israel bought their tithes and offerings into the storehouse *again*, so that the temple workers could return to work. In this case, the rebuke of Malachi 3 is not at all directed toward the people who were failing to tithe, but upon a priest and his friends who were not using the tithe properly but were selling it or hoarding it all for themselves. They were not giving the full portion that was due to those who worked and ministered in the temple. It was certain priests, not the people, who were robbing from God and from the nation.

This puts the message of Malachi 3 in a different light, does it not? The rebuke is directed at the spiritual leaders for their misuse and mishandling of the tithe which had been brought by the people. The rebuke was directed at the priests; not at the people.

Now if the people had failed to bring in the tithe, could the rebuke have been directed at them? I suppose it could have been. Yet in such a situation, would God have said that the people were robbing Him? Probably not. The language of the rebuke might have still contained elements of blessing for obedience and cursing for disobedience as these were consequences stated within the law (Deut 28), but it is doubtful that God would have accused the people of robbing Him in the same way that He was accusing the priests. Failing to give to God is not robbing God, but once money and resources have been set aside for ministry purposes, to use this money for selfish or personal gain is robbing God. This is what some priests were doing, which is why they were rebuked for robbing God. Therefore, Malachi 3:8-10 is a rebuke of disobedient priests for stealing the tithes and offerings of the people.

If there is a proper application of this text today, it would be better to direct it to the religious leaders in our churches, rather than to the people in the pews. The message to the priests and pastors would be to ask them how they are spending the tithes and offerings of the people, and whether these offerings are being used for their intended purpose: to take care of the pastor's needs (if he is really equivalent to a Levitical priest), to feed the hungry in the community, and to look after orphans and widows in need (Deut 26:12).

Does the passage have any real application for people today who do not tithe, or who give less than the traditional 10% (which is really only 3%, as we saw in a previous section)? Not really.

Even if it the text was directed at the people rather than the priests, the blessing for obedience and cursing for disobedience were consequences for *the people of Israel living under the Mosaic Law*. Followers of Jesus are not under the Law of Moses. We are under the Law of Christ, the Law of Freedom and Liberty (Gal 6:2; Jas 2:12). As such, everything we own belongs to God, and He does want us to use what we have and what we earn to help advance His Kingdom through generous giving and by loving and serving others. This is what Jesus and the rest of the New Testament Scriptures teach about giving, and it is to these Scriptures we now turn.

What Jesus Taught About Tithing. Jesus didn't talk a lot about tithing, and when He did, it was usually in a negative context. For example, in Matthew 23:23 (and Luke 11:42), Jesus indicated that the Pharisees and religious leaders were overly concerned with giving an exact 10% of everything, even down to measuring 10% of the spices of mint, anise, and cumin. Jesus goes on to encourage the leaders to continue giving, but tells them to focus more of their devotion and energy to things that matter, like justice, mercy, and faith.

The only other time that Jesus specifically mentioned tithing was when He contrasted a self-righteous and legalistic religious leader with a humble and repentant tax-collector (Luke 18:11-12). It was the religious Pharisee who was concerned with giving the exact 10% of his income to God who was criticized by Jesus, while the repentant tax-collector received the praise of Jesus. It is unknown what actions this repentant tax-collector performed as a result of his repentance, but if he was anything like Zacchaeus, he may have given away 50% of his fortune to the poor, and returned 400% of any money he had taken from people through extortion (Luke 19:8). Notice that Zacchaeus doesn't give the money to the temple, but to the people who needed it and to the people he had stolen from. It is likely that this repentant tax-collector in Luke 18 did something similar.

From these passages, it appears that Jesus is not as concerned about people giving money to the temple, or how much they give, as He is concerned with the more important matters of justice for the oppressed, mercy to the repentant, and faith toward God in all things. When religious groups and leaders focus on making sure everybody tithes 10%, they are showing signs of legalism and self-righteousness, and are often guilty of things God *really* is concerned about, such as justice, mercy, love, and faith.

This seems to be the general thrust of the teaching from Jesus about tithing. Giving is never discouraged, and the goal in giving is not to give a certain amount but to give in ways that rights wrongs, restores justice, helps the poor, and encourages dependence upon God. When it comes to giving, Jesus is more concerned with the motive than the amount.

Nevertheless, there are two passages in the Gospels that are often used to teach the idea that Jesus was concerned about the percentage that people give. These two passages are where Jesus is asked about paying taxes to Caesar, and when Jesus observes a poor widow giving her last two coins to the temple. What do these two passages say (and not say) about Jesus' view of tithing?

Give to Caesar what is Caesar's. Matthew 22:21 is sometimes used to defend the practice of tithing. In response to a question about whether the Jews should pay taxes or not, Jesus says, "Render therefore to Caesar the things that are Caesar's, and to God the things that are God's." It is sometimes taught that since in the first part of this verse Jesus affirms the responsibility to pay taxes to Caesar, the second part of the verse affirms the responsibility to pay "taxes" to God in the form of tithes.

This application, however, is not the best way of understanding what Jesus says. The passage begins with the Pharisees wanting to tangle and entrap Jesus (Matt 22:15). So they send some of their disciples and some Herodians to ask Jesus a trick question (Matt 22:16). These two groups represent two of the many factions within Israel at this time. The Pharisees were often sympathetic to the segment of Jewish people who wanted the Roman occupation of Israel to cease and thought that no law should rule in Israel except God's law as found in the Torah. The Herodians, however, were supporters of King Herod, who was a vassal king of the Roman Emperor. King Herod was placed into power by the Emperor, and was given numerous privileges in Israel as long as he upheld the peace and worked to maintain Roman governance over the region. As supporters of King Herod, the Herodians also gained access to some of the privileges that the Emperor had bestowed upon Herod.

And now these two factions have come to Jesus to see which side He will take. It is not that these two factions have unified against Jesus. Rather, they have come to Jesus to have him settle their dispute, and each side is ready to pounce upon Jesus if He opposes their view. So they ask Jesus whether or not it is lawful to pay taxes to Caesar (Matt 22:16-17).

If Jesus says it is not lawful, then He sides with the Pharisees and with the majority of the people of Israel. Many believed that paying taxes to Roman Emperor was idolatrous since he claimed to be god, and since the Roman Empire spent tax money on many things that the Jewish people considered to be evil. Of course, if Jesus sides with the Pharisees while the Herodians are there, then they will go back and tell King Herod what Jesus said, and the King would most likely have Jesus arrested for refusing to pay taxes and inciting rebellion among the people.

If, however, Jesus sided with the Herodians in saying that the people should pay taxes to Caesar, then this would be viewed by the religious leaders and the majority of the Jewish people as both idolatrous and traitorous, as it would be seen as placing Roman law above God's law and telling people to support the wicked and wasteful spending of the Roman Empire.

It seems like a perfect trap. Jesus is faced with a nearly impossible dilemma. If He sides with the people, He faces imprisonment and death. If He sides with the Herodians, He loses His support among the people and His standing as a righteous rabbinical leader.

What does Jesus do? He asks for a denarius. The denarius was the amount of the tax in question, and in asking for the coin, Jesus begins to reveal some of the hypocrisy of the religious leaders. Some of the religious leaders taught that it was a sin to even carry such a coin, as it bore the image of Caesar, and was thus viewed as a graven image. Having such a coin was interpreted by some as breaking the second commandment (Exod 20:4). However, the passage is unclear about where the coin came from—maybe it came from the Herodians—and so this is not the main hypocrisy that Jesus is concerned with.

Upon being given the coin, Jesus asks whose image is on it, and they answer "Caesar's." It is then that He tells them, "Render therefore to Caesar the things that are Caesar's, and to God the things that are God's." Some have tried to explain Jesus' words by saying that His answer was ambivalent about taxes. They understand Jesus to be saying, "Give to Caesar what he's got coming," which is almost a veiled threat. But it seems best to understand the text at face value: Jesus believes that people to pay taxes to Caesar. And if this is where Jesus had stopped, Jesus would have essentially been throwing His support in with the Herodians.

But He does not stop. He goes on to say the people should give "to God the things that are God's." What "things" does Jesus have in mind? Again, some think that since Jesus was talking about paying taxes to Caesar, then Jesus must still have money in mind and is now saying that people must also pay taxes to God in the form of giving tithes to the temple. In this case, Jesus would be saying, "Pay taxes to Caesar, and tithes to God, and in this way, obey both the laws of man and of God."

Jesus means something else, however. He is not talking about tithing at all. No, Jesus clearly drew a connection between the image that was on the coin and His answer that since Caesar's image was on the coin, it must belong to Caesar. So when Jesus talking about giving to God what belongs to God, the question that people are to ask is, "If things that bear Caesar's image belong to Caesar, then God must get those things that bear God's image." And what is it that bears the image of God? We do. Human beings bear the image of God.

The Greek word Jesus uses for "image" in Matthew 22:20 (Gk., *eikōn*), is the same word used for "image" in the Greek translation of Genesis 1:26 when God says, "Let us make man in our image." So when Jesus says, "Give to God what is God's" He is not talking about money at all, but about giving ourselves to God. And this really is the point of Jesus. The Pharisees were concerned that giving a coin to Caesar might somehow be a form of idolatry or breaking God's law. Jesus' solution is to go ahead and give Caesar his money, if that is what he wants. But Jesus then points out that God doesn't want our money; He wants us. Caesar can have his little piece of metal with his image stamped on it, for God has stamped His image upon what He wants: us.

In this way, Jesus faithfully and accurately answered the trick question of the Herodians and Pharisees, letting each party feel as if He has sided with them, while at the same time leaving no room for the Herodians to accuse Him of inciting rebellion, and leaving the Pharisees no room to accuse Him of idolatry. Yet, as we have seen, Jesus really didn't side with either group, but instead challenged both groups to rethink the role of money. They were arguing about money, and in a subversive sort of way, Jesus shows that money (and arguments about money) are relatively worthless. If Caesar wants a bit of metal with his face stamped on it, give it to him. What really matters, says Jesus, is how we live our lives for God.

As long as we are loving and serving God with all our heart, soul, mind, and strength, we can obey the laws of our government and those in authority over us without fear of falling into idolatry and sin. As long as God has all of us, He does not care if we give little bits of metal and paper to human authorities to do with what they want. They will be responsible to God for how they rule; we are responsible to God for how we live. So, give to Caesar what is Caesar's, and give to God what is God's.

So this incident, while instructive about our use of money, says nothing about whether or not we should pay tithes.

The Widow's Mites. By far the most famous passage in the Gospels about tithing is the account of the widow's mites. The account is found in Mark 12:41-44 and Luke 21:1-4. Jesus and His disciples are in the temple, observing people bring their tithes and offerings. They observed the rich giving large amounts of money and then saw a poor widow giving two mites. These were very small copper coins, which today would be equivalent to a few pennies. She did not give much at all. And yet, Jesus says that she gave more than all the rich, for they gave out of their wealth, while out of her poverty she gave her last few coins.

This is a popular passage in sermons and teachings on tithing, and is often taught with two main points. First, we are told that this passage teaches that Jesus is not so concerned with the amount a person gives, but with the percentage. It is likely that the rich people in the temple were tithing a full 10% of their income, and as a result, were giving huge sums of money to the temple. However, they still owned 90% of their wealth. The poor widow, on the other hand, though she only gave two mites, gave 100% of what she had, and kept nothing for herself. So, we are told that the amount we give to God is not as important as the percentage.

The second point often made from this Scripture is that God wants even the poor to tithe, and to tithe generously. The widow, though she had almost nothing, gave what she had, and Jesus praised her for it. We are then told that even if we are debt, even if we are poor, even if we cannot afford to pay our bills, even if we have lost our jobs and our homes, we still need to make sure we tithe to God before anything else.

Sermons that make this second point about poor people tithing often transition over to Matthew 19:29 (or Mark 10:29-30) where Jesus promises that those who give up relationships, possessions, homes, and land for His sake, will receive one-hundred times as much in this life and in the life to come. The intended message is that if you are poor or having trouble paying your bills, make sure you give the first portion of your income to God, because that will open the storehouses of heaven, and you will receive a hundred times more than what you give. This poor woman who gave all she had received the commendation and blessing of Jesus.

But is this really what the passage is teaching? Is it teaching that God cares more about the percentage we give than the actual amount, and that even poor people should give out of their poverty?

No.

The passage teaches nothing of the sort. Jesus is not condemning the rich people for being wealthy or for giving out of their wealth, nor is He praising the poor widow for giving her last two mites. To the contrary, the context seems to indicate that Jesus is saddened by the entire scene.

The surrounding context of this passage sheds light on how Jesus felt about what was going on in the temple that day. In Mark 12, right before Jesus observes and comments upon the rich giving from their wealth and the widow giving from her poverty, Jesus condemns the religious leaders for their pride, arrogance, self-prominence, and greed. In highlighting their greed, Jesus says that they "devour widows' houses" (Mark 12:40). According to the Law of Moses, the spiritual leaders were supposed to be taking care of the widows and orphans in the community, and providing for their needs (Deut 26:12). But here they are doing the opposite. They are taking away from the widows what little they have left, leaving them destitute, without even a home to live in.

Could it really be that only three verses later, Jesus is now praising the sacrifice of a widow for giving her last two coins to the temple? How can this be? The temple should be giving to her; not her to the temple! They have already taken her house, and now they take her last two coins as well! Jesus is not happy and encouraged by what He sees, but saddened. He is not upset at the poor woman. Far from it! He is upset and saddened at how far the worship of God in the temple has degenerated that the priests and Levites are teaching and even demanding that poor widows who have no homes and no income give up their last two coins to support the work of the Lord.

If we read Mark 12:43-44 again with this perspective in mind, we see that Jesus is not amazed and impressed at this poor widow's courage and faith, but is almost choking back the tears at how this woman has been caught in the lies of greedy deception by the rich and wealthy religious leaders. She is only doing what she has been told. She obeys out of faith, knowing that her sacrifice is probably her death sentence. But she loves God so much, she does it anyway. Her actions are not her fault. It is the religious leaders who are at fault. They have devoured her house and now they are taking her life as well. Asking widows to tithe from their poverty is like using religion to pick the pockets of the poor. The temple should have been giving money to her in her time of need; not the other way around (cf. 1 Tim 5:3-16).

Earlier in His ministry, Jesus had also criticized the religious leaders for teaching people that it was their priority to give to the temple if such giving deprived a person's family of financial support (Mark 7:10-13). Jesus taught, along with the Mosaic Law, that one's primary responsibility was to support their family. If it was wrong for a person to tithe to the temple while neglecting their family, it would also be wrong to ask poverty-stricken widows to give to the temple, when they had no one to provide for them. This was especially true if this widow had children which she needed to support.

Here is what John Pilch says about this passage:

Jesus does not praise but rather laments this woman's behavior. She has been taught "sacrificial giving" by her religious leaders, and that is the pity. These authorities promised to redistribute Temple collections to the needy. In actuality, they spent the funds on conspicuous consumption instead: long robes and banquets. This is how they "devoured the estates of widows."[14]

If this is the case with the widow, what did Jesus think about the wealthy people giving to the temple? It seems that He was not in favor of them giving to the temple either. Jesus is not too concerned about their wealth (except that maybe some of them had gained their riches through devouring widow's houses), nor even with how much they are giving. Jesus is primarily concerned with the fact that they are giving it *to the temple*. Here is this poor widow in their midst, who has no home, and has only two pennies left to her name, and all the wealthy people are generously giving to the temple, when they should be giving some of their money to her. I think that Jesus would say that this widow is more important than any temple.

Immediately after this event, the disciples of Jesus ask Jesus about the temple, and Jesus says it is all going to be destroyed (Mark 13:1-2). It is beyond imagination that Jesus could be praising anybody for giving money of any amount to a building and institution that was about to be destroyed! It is much better, Jesus would say, to give to the poor, the needy, and destitute, than to a building and religious system that was about to be destroyed.

The triple tragedy of this account is that the rich were giving money where it was not needed, the widow was giving money she didn't have, and the spiritual leaders were using religion to enrich themselves off both. The ideal situation, it

---

[14] John J. Pilch, *The Cultural World of Jesus: Cycle B* (Collegeville, MA: Liturgical, 1996), 162.

seems, would have been for the widow to keep her mites, for the rich to see her desperate situation and provide for her in her time of need, and for the religious leaders to bless both people for their decisions and be content with what they had.

So what application can we pull from this passage? First, let us consider the spiritual leaders. They hold the greatest guilt in this text, and if there is any outrage at all from Jesus in this passage, it is directed toward them. It is they who were devouring widow's houses, and teaching both the rich and poor alike to give of their money to the temple for "God's work," when in reality, the money went for their own stomachs and closets. The application for spiritual leaders today is obvious: Do not place scriptural and theological guilt trips on people to make them think that God wants their money. He doesn't. If you are going to teach people to "give to God," lead by example in giving of your own money to the poor in your community, and also invite the people under your care to give to whatever needs they are aware of, whether or not it helps pay the bills of the church or your own salary.

Secondly, there is application here for the poor. Those who are struggling to pay their bills and are living in poverty should never be expected to give money to religious institutions. Their God-given priorities are for the health and well-being of their own family. Period. Yes, there may be budgeting, money management, stewardship, personal discipline, and workplace ethical issues which may be part of the reason some people are poor. But teaching and training in these areas are things the church can (and should) provide to the poor *while* the church provides for the needs of the poor. Never should the church tell the poor that they are poor because they don't give enough money "to God." When speaking to the self-righteous rich of His own day, Jesus told them to sell all they had and give it to the poor (Matt 19:21; Luke 12:33; 18:22). This is what He would tell the rich churches and wealthy church leaders of our own day as well.

Finally, there is some application for wealthy people. Jesus nowhere condemns their wealth. It is not a sin to be wealthy. Also, it does not appear that Jesus is too concerned about the amount of money they give. It seems more likely from the context that Jesus is concerned about *what* they were giving to. They were giving to a corrupt and condemned institution where the funds were spent not on taking care of the poor and needy in the community, but on providing fancy clothes and sumptuous feasts for the spiritual leaders.

Yet even though Jesus seems to be ambivalent about how much money these wealthy people had and how much of it they were giving to the temple (which was probably 10%), this does not mean that Jesus had nothing to say on the subject. One of the primary topics in the teaching of Jesus is money and what people should do with it. And most often, Jesus teaches that those who have more money should give it to those who have less. But in no case does Jesus ever equate this sort of giving to "tithing." Giving to the poor and those in need is just simply what God expects from those who have more. Giving to the poor is an act of Christian love and generosity. It is what Jesus expects from those who follow Him.

Not surprisingly then, this generosity toward others is what we encounter in the rest of the New Testament as the early church is founded and as Paul travels around planting churches and providing instruction to these churches on how to live and function as followers of Jesus Christ.

Giving in the Early Church. As we read about the early church and how they handled money, one of the first examples we come to, and also the most famous, is the account in Acts 4:32–5:11. The text begins by stating that nobody in the community was in need because those who had more shared with those who had less. One example is given where a man named

Barnabas sells some of his property and gives the money to the apostles who then distribute it to those within the church who had need (Acts 4:32-37).

Following this, in Acts 5, we read about a husband and wife in the church named Ananias and Sapphira, who decide to do something similar. They also sell some of their possessions, with the intention of giving the proceeds to the church. But when they receive the money, rather than give everything, they only gave part of the proceeds. However, they tell the apostles and the rest of the church that they had given everything. As a result, both of them are struck dead by the Holy Spirit (Acts 5:1-11).

It is worth being reminded that the sin of Ananias and Sapphira was not in their failure to give everything they are earned, but in lying to the church (and to God) about giving everything they had earned. We must not read into this passage anything about a requirement to give 100% of our profit to the church. To the contrary, Ananias and Sapphira were not required to give any of the profit from their land sale to the church if they did not want to. It would have been perfectly legitimate for them to have sold their possessions and kept 100% of the money for themselves.

They had apparently seen how much praise and honor Barnabas received when he sold his property and gave the money to help those in need, and wanted to get similar praise and honor for themselves. This was the wrong motive for giving, and then on top of it, they lied about how much they had received in the sale, and how much they were giving to the church.

It is also worth noting what the early church was doing with the money they received from those who so generously gave to the church. The context indicates that the money went to provide for anyone who had need (Acts 2:45-56; 4:32-35; 6:1). By all appearances, there were no buildings or paid staff or expensive programs. The money collected from those who had excess went to support the daily needs of those who had less. This is an incredibly important concept for how we should operate in our own giving, and what the church can do with the money it receives from donors. We will look at this concept later in the chapter.

For now, let us turn to one final passage in the New Testament which is often preached upon during sermon series on tithing and giving to the local church.

Generous and Joyful Giving. The central chapters in the New Testament about giving are 2 Corinthians 8–9. In these chapters Paul provides his suggestions on who should give, how much they should give, what they should give to, why they should give, and how the church should use what is given.

Note first of all that not once in these chapters do we read about tithing. Paul is not writing about the Christian tithe. He is not interested in resurrecting or reworking the instructions about tithing from the Mosaic Law. He recognized, as we have seen above, that the laws about tithing were for Jewish people living in a covenant relationship with the God of Israel, and with the temple and the priestly Levitical system as one of the central symbols of that covenant. There was no command from Paul for the Corinthian believers to give 10% or any other percentage. There is not even a command *to* give. To the contrary, he explicitly states that what he writes is "not by commandment" (2 Cor 8:9). Instead, he was urging them to finish what they had already started.

What was it they had started? There were several Macedonian churches in deep poverty, and the Corinthian church offered to help these other churches out financially (2 Cor 8:2). Being in deep poverty does not mean that these churches were unable to pay their pastor, or were falling behind on their mortgage. No, remember that such things did not exist at that time. When Paul says that these churches were facing affliction and were in deep poverty, he means that the people themselves could not afford food and clothing. Many of them had probably lost their jobs as a result of becoming Christians. Some of the men had probably been imprisoned, or even killed, leaving their wives and children without income and support.

And so now, Paul is exhorting some of the churches who were not experiencing similar difficulties, to give from their excess to the churches which were facing such dire need. When a church in one area faced persecution and poverty, churches in another area not only prayed for them and sent people to support these other churches, but also sent gifts of money to provide food and clothing for those who could not afford it (cf. Acts 11:27-30; 1 Cor 16:1-4; Gal 2:10).

As an example, Paul points to Jesus Christ who gave up the riches of heaven to become poor for the sake of the earth, so that through His poverty we might become rich (2 Cor 8:9). Paul encourages the Corinthian believers to follow the same example, to give from their riches so that those who are poor might have their needs met. Paul does not want the Corinthians to be burdened, but wants them to share out of their abundance to provide for those who are lacking so that there is equality (2 Cor 8:13-15).

So in exhorting the Corinthians to give, he tells them to give freely, to give joyfully, and to give generously (2 Cor 9). Each person can give what they have decided in their own heart to give. There is no recommended percentage or suggested donation amount. But through their giving, they will sow seeds of righteousness that will multiply and produce fruit of thanksgiving and glory to God. Followers of Jesus are encouraged to give, but to give in such a way that supports the poor and the needy. This teaching exactly matches that of Jesus, and the entire rest of the Bible on how to use our money for God's work.

No Texts on Tithing. There is nothing in Scripture which demands or commands the Christians tithe. The Israelites were commanded to tithe, but this is because they lived in a theocra-

95

cy, and the tithe functioned as a tax. It supported the priestly leadership of the nation, helped the individual families enjoy life with one another, and provided the means to support the poor and needy in the community.

As follow of Jesus, we are not under a theocracy, have no designated priestly class (for in Christ, we are all "priests"–1 Pet 2:9), and while we still do pay taxes, we pay them to whatever government we find ourselves in. We are free to use our money in whatever way we see fit, knowing of course, that all we have comes from God, and as needs arise, we should make our resources available to help accomplish the work of God in this world, and provide for the poor in the community.

So if there is one overarching, guiding principle in Scripture about how God wants us to use our money, it is that those who have more should provide for those who have less. This principle is found in the Mosaic Law instructions to the Israelites about tithing, in the teaching and example of Jesus, and in the teaching and example of the early church in the book of Acts and the letter of the Apostles to the churches. We have no command to tithe, but we do have instructions and exhortations to give of our resources to help those who are in need. The poor should not be expected to give to churches and ministries and spiritual leaders, but should be receiving aid from these organizations and leaders instead.

With this is as the instruction and example from Scripture, let us turn to look at some practical suggestions for how churches and individuals can use their money to advance the Kingdom of God and support those in our communities and around the world who are in need.

THE CHURCH THAT GIVES

One of the basic things that a church could do with the money they receive for the advancement of the Kingdom of God and the support of the poor and needy in the community is to become a church that gives. Rather than spending the majority of our income on buildings, salaries, and church programs so that only what is left over goes to help the poor and needy, maybe churches could reverse this practice so that a majority of the money a church receives goes toward feeding the hungry, helping the poor, and serving those who are outcast and rejected in society.

Though there is no hard and fast rule, it seems that if loving and serving others really is a priority for the church, the church budget could reflect this by setting aside a majority (51% or more) of the church income for service-oriented ministry. Such a move would be impossible for most established churches, but they could begin moving in this direction by portioning off an ever-increasing percentage of their annual budget for serving the community in this way.

I am aware of several churches that actually do this, but most of them are in the mega-church category and have annual operating budgets of $5 million or more. These churches often pride themselves in giving 51% of their budget to "missions." This is wonderful, and is to be encouraged and praised. Yet I sometimes think that for churches like these, 51% is not nearly enough. It's like the man who makes $5 million a year saying he tithes 51%. This is wonderful, but they are still living off $2.5 million per year. There is definite room for improvement. So also with mega churches. Though they may be giving millions of dollars to missions, they spend tens of thousands of dollars a year on air-conditioning an empty building, new choir robes, colorful bulletins, professional cleaning for the padded pews, and numerous other relatively unnecessary items.

Furthermore, when you begin to look at the 51% of the money that goes toward "missions" it is sometimes shocking to discover how loosely some churches define "missions." Oftentimes, the church will have a "Mission Pastor" whose salary comes out of the mission's budget. Frequently, the church will subsidize the expenses for the youth group to go on several "mission trips" per year, which usually amount to little more than a sight-seeing trip. I know of one mega church that boasts about how they give 51% of their income to missions, but out of their budget, they pay for all the housing and living expenses for half-a-dozen "stateside missionaries." I definitely agree that the Unites States need people to live the gospel and share it with others, but I am not sure that it is a good use of church funds to pay people a full-time salary so they can be missionaries to the United States. I mean, if the people we are trying to reach are out working in business offices and factories, wouldn't it make sense for the "stateside missionary" to also work a job at a business office or factory? As it turns out, with this one church I am familiar with, very little of the 51% of the church budget for "missions" goes toward serving the poor and helping the needy in the community or around the world.

New church plants could lead the way in this regard. They could make it a habit from day one that over 50% of their budget will go to loving and serving people. So no matter what new expense the church plant wanted to incur, they would need to double it before deciding whether it was worth the money. If they want to hire a pastor for $60,000, he will actually cost $120,000. If they want to construct a building which will have a monthly mortgage payment of $5000, it will actually cost $10,000. Planning the church budget in this way really makes church leaders and elders think twice about where they spend their money, and whether or not it is really necessary to pave the parking lot or upgrade the sound system.

The first church I pastored was very small, and so we were naturally trying to attract more people to the church. At the time, I was very jealous of First Baptist Church in town, because they had the gleaming building, the perfect lawn, and a huge, nicely paved parking lot. Our building was a little run down, the lawn was covered in weeds, and we had a gravel parking lot. So one year, we decided that it would be good to use most of our church savings on paving the parking lot. We spent just over $10,000 to turn our gravel parking lot into a nice, paved parking lot. Over the course of the next year, how many people did we add to the church? Not one.

Looking back, I often wonder what would have happened if we had spent that money helping out several single mothers in the community instead. We wouldn't have even had to go looking for them; we knew several who were in dire need. Or maybe we could have brought food over to families where the father was out of work. Again, there were several families on the very street on which the church sat who were having trouble putting food on the table. Or we could have created a job training center in one of the unused back rooms of the church. The ministry and service options we *could have* done were nearly endless, but instead we paved the parking lot. I sometimes wonder how that parking lot looks today.

In his book, *The Next Christians,* Gabe Lyons writes about how churches are beginning to ask different questions about money. Rather than ask, "How can we spend money to increase our programs, beautify our building, or improve our worship experience?" they are asking, "How can we serve for the good of the city—no strings attached?"[15] He goes on to provide numerous examples of churches that set up free community health and dental clinics, adopt public schools for child mentoring, provide food and shelter for homeless families, and numerous other approaches of loving and serving the community in tangible ways with money that could have been spent elsewhere.

Churches need to see that the way we give back to the community is by giving back to the community. We don't give back to the community by paving our parking lot, having a

---

[15] Gabe Lyons, *The Next Christians* (New York: Doubleday, 2010), 182-183.

manicured lawn, and buying a state-of-the-art sound system. If a group of believers wants to own a building and pay a pastor, this isn't necessarily wrong, as long as they make these of secondary importance. When Christians in the New Testament are exhorted to give (and this is true of the Israel with their tithe as well), it is primarily for the purpose of supporting the poor and needy both locally and around the world. These sorts of things should be the budget priority of any church group or gathering.

CHURCH BUDGET PLANNING WITH JESUS

How then should our church budgets be organized to accomplish the most good for the Kingdom of God? Jesus might have something to say to us about this.

If Jesus were to show up at the annual meeting of the typical church, He would probably sit in the back and wait for the pastor or one of the elders to ask His opinion on the church budget. If they did, He might say, "You should organize your budget so that people do not commit adultery, do not murder, do not steal, do not bear false witness, and honor their father and mother."

And the church elders would glance smugly at each other and answer Jesus, saying, "Good Teacher. This is what we have been doing for many years! People have been trained. Disciples have been made. Hatred is being replaced with love. Marriages have been helped. Men are loving their wives, and wives are respecting their husbands. Youth and teens are being taught to honor and obey their parents. And as a result of all this, God has blessed our church! Membership is up thirty percent, we paid off our mortgage last year, and we are looking at purchasing some prime real estate across town to launch a satellite campus. These are things we have been doing since the birth of this church."

When Jesus hears these things, He would probably look at them and say, "You still lack one thing. Sell all you have, and distribute your money to the poor."

The suggestion of Jesus would get put before the people for discussion. Most of the people who get up to speak would remind everybody how hard everyone had worked as a church to get where they were, and how many people made great sacrifices to achieve their success. The pastor had even been asked to speak at a national church conference next year, and it was rumored that a book deal was in the works. If they sold everything and gave all the money away, what would happen to everything they had worked so hard for? Where would the people worship? How would they do ministry without a building? How could they serve without any money? Sure, they might be able to help some poor people, but once the money ran out, then what?

A vote would be called for, and seconded, and when put to vote, the motion would fail unanimously. The elders would look back to where Jesus had been sitting gauge His reaction, only to find out He was no longer there. Sometime during the discussion about the church's success, Jesus had slipped out the back door, probably to hang out with the homeless in the alley around the corner.

You have probably heard that story before. In the Gospels, when a rich young ruler comes to Jesus to ask how to inherit eternal life, Jesus tells him that he must sell all he has and give the money to the poor (Luke 18:18-23). Despite how this passage is sometimes used in sermons and books as an attempt to get the rich to give more money to the church, the point of this passage actually lies elsewhere.

In Jewish ways of thinking, much like today, money and wealth were signs of God's grace and blessing. The Mosaic Law promised that if a person obeyed God and followed the Covenant, then God would bless them with land, crops, cattle, peace, prosperity, and health (Deut 28:1-14). If, however, someone did not have all these things, then it was a sign that they (or their ancestors) were sinful and had rebelled against God, and God was punishing them as a result (Deut 28:15-68).

So when Jesus told the rich man to keep the entire law, it seems arrogant and preposterous to us today for the man to respond as he did, that he had kept the entire law since he was a boy. But from a Jewish perspective, the evidence was clear: Look how rich he was! God's grace was irrefutably upon him. Again, this is much like today in our churches. We tend to believe that if a church become large and wealthy, it is evidence that God's grace is upon them and they must be doing most things right. After all, look how much God has blessed them!

It is only after the man claims to have kept the whole law that Jesus turns the tables on him. He tells the rich young ruler to sell all he has and give the money to the poor. Even here, we must be careful to properly understand the text. Jesus is not really concerned with what the man does with his wealth. Instead, Jesus is concerned with how the man views himself as a result of his wealth, and how he views the poor as a result of their lack of wealth.

The man viewed his wealth as evidence of God's grace upon him, and viewed the lack of wealth among the poor as evidence that they were rebellious sinners. By telling the man to give all his wealth to the poor, Jesus was essentially telling him to give up all his evidence of God's love and grace, and give all that evidence of love and grace to those the man considered to be wicked and rebellious sinners. In this circumstance, the rich man, having become penniless, would be viewed by others as having come under the judgment and condemnation of God.

This is why the man went away sad. He did not want to give up the evidence of God's grace upon him, especially not to those whom he felt were undeserving. Jesus was trying to point out to the rich young ruler that in God's economy, all are blessed, all are welcome, all are accepted. The rich and the poor alike are on equal footing before God. Those whom we think are within the grace of God, and those we judge as being outside of God's grace are often exactly backwards from God's perspective. Though we may deny it, many Christians do in fact feel that God blesses obedience with riches and wealth, and He disciplines the disobedient with poverty.

Philip J. Lee noticed this tendency himself, and wrote this about it in his book, *Against the Protestant Gnostics:*

> Henry Ward Beecher, one of the most popular preachers of his day, was quite in line with Protestant thought when he declared, "Looking comprehensively through city and town and village and country, the general truth will stand, that no man in this land suffers from poverty unless it be more than his fault—unless it be his sin." It is little wonder that in 1874 Beecher could say, without embarrassment, "Our churches are largely for the mutual insurance of prosperous families, and not for the upbuilding of the great underclass of humanity." In the same year, the Rev. Charles Wood with similar indifference, observed, "The poor are not provided for, nor are they wanted as part of the congregations which worship in the majority of our city churches."[16]

Many churches view their buildings, possessions, and prestige in the community the same way the rich young ruler of Luke 18 viewed his vast wealth. They see their riches as a sign of God's grace and blessing upon them. If they give such things away to the poor, there will be nothing left to provide evidence of God's grace.

To be honest, Jesus probably wasn't so concerned with the wealth the rich young ruler had, and He probably isn't overly

---

[16] Philip J. Lee, *Against the Protestant Gnostics* (New York: Oxford, 1987), 167.

concerned about the buildings that churches own today. His primary concern is with how these possessions are viewed, and what we do with what we have, especially for those who do not have as much. Jesus wanted to challenge the whole way of thinking which says, "Those who have more are loved more; and those who have less are loved less."

Could it be that God has given some people more than others, not so that they can feel extra special, become puffed up about how great of people they are in God's eyes, or how wonderful their ministries are for the advancement of the Kingdom of God, but so that those to whom God has given more can use what they have to bless others who have been given less, and in so doing, be blessed in other ways in return? Could it be that wealth distribution has nothing to do with righteousness, morality, and God's blessing, but has everything to do with God's plan to make a people of God for Himself where everybody works together and provides for one another in a vast array of interconnected friendships and mutually dependent relationships? After all, the physically poor often have spiritual, emotional, and relational wealth which those who are physically rich know nothing about.

When the rich give to the poor, they soon discover that the poor give more back to them. No, not in the form of wealth and prosperity, but in the form of joy, peace, and fulfillment. So those who are rich should seek to distribute some of their wealth to the poor, for this is how God planned it. God gives us money, not so we can build bigger buildings, resurface our parking lot, and expand our online presence. He gives us money so we can give it to others. As Shane Claiborne says, "Giving to the poor should not make its way into the budget; it *is* the budget."[17]

---

[17] Shane Claiborne, *Irresistible Revolution* (Grand Rapids: Zondervan, 2006), 330.

If this is beginning to sound suspiciously like the political hot-topic of the redistribution of wealth, that's because it is. However, redistribution of wealth was God's idea first. When governments try to accomplish it, they always fail. Wealth redistribution must be done God's way or not at all.

REDISTRIBUTION OF WEALTH

Earlier in this chapter we discussed the giving pattern of the early church. In that discussion it was seen that those who had more sold their possessions so that the money could be distributed to those who had less (cf. Acts 2:45-56; 4:32-35; 6:1). This is the true biblical model of "redistributing the wealth."

But notice what is not involved anywhere in this redistribution: the government. Redistribution of wealth is a wonderful idea, is commended by God, and there are numerous examples of it within the pages of Scripture, some of which we have looked at above. But wealth redistribution is not something that can be commanded, required, or legislated. You cannot create laws which are enforced by the government to take money from the rich and give it to the poor. This has never worked in the history of the world, and never will. Why? Because if the rich want to remain rich, then threatening to take their riches will only cause them to hide it better, or cause them to find other ways to become even more rich than before. Whenever a government tries to legislate the redistribution of wealth, the only ones who suffer are the poor.

Furthermore, not all the poor deserve the aid that is offered. There are some among the poor who could and should be working, but since they get free handouts from the government, they refuse to work or even to look for a job. When the rich see their money going to people who could be providing for themselves but aren't, they are usually not too happy about the money they give, and they definitely don't want to give more.

The great problem with governments and economic systems that are built upon the wealthy supporting the poor is that they masquerade as being the biblical model. They often claim that they are only trying to take care of the poor as taught and practiced by Jesus and the early church. But nothing could be further from the truth.

Communism, socialism, and every government-run economic plan to redistribute wealth, functions on the principle of taking money from the rich and giving it to the poor. The government often serves as the mediator in this transaction by taxing the rich, and then running the money through a vast array of bureaucracies until eventually, a small portion of what was given finally makes it to the nameless masses of poor people, many of whom do not even need the aid, could otherwise work but choose not to, or are taking advantage of the system. This process is full of waste, fraud, and abuse. Furthermore, as the wealthy see what is going on, they feel like the government is stealing from them, and most the poor are not really helped in the long term, but only become ever more dependent upon the government for financial aid.

The biblical model, which is the model practiced by Jesus and by the early church in Acts, is very different. There truly was redistribution of wealth, but it did not depend on a government agency to step in and take money from the rich. It did not depend on threats and taxation. The money that was given did not get lost in leaky bureaucrat accounts and the broken cogs of government. The money from the rich did not go to the underserving and the lazy. In the biblical model of wealth redistribution, the money went to help people who had genuine needs, and it actually helped them rise above their situation so that they no longer needed help, and most amazingly of all, the wealthy never felt cheated, robbed, or taken advantage of. They felt it was a joy and privilege to bless others in such tangible ways.

What was this biblical system of wealth redistribution? It was called generosity. The current governmental systems encourage the poor to say, "What's yours is mine." But the biblical example taught the rich to say, "What's mine is yours." The rich were encouraged and challenged to give as much as they could as often as they could to help those less fortunate and to help those who faced difficult life situations.

There are numerous factors that allow some people to get rich. Sometimes money is inherited, and sometimes it genuinely results for good ideas and hard work. But frequently, becoming wealthy is a matter of luck and being in the right place at the right time. It is usually also true that those who are rich have learned to make wise decisions with their money. Nevertheless, however one becomes rich, they typically do not appreciate being forced to give their income to people who do not work or who have made poor decisions with their money. But many rich people love to use some of their money to help other people, especially when it goes for a good cause, to help people out of a bad situation, or even to provide life skills and job training that will lift other people out of their situation.

But this sort of generosity on the part of the rich often requires personal involvement and the development of relationships between the rich and the poor. And since the two groups of people usually live and function in completely different circles, it is difficult to bring the two groups together. But this is one area where churches are unusually effective. With some intentional planning and organization, churches can create space and time for the rich to help the poor and the poor to bless the rich. The church can be the great equalizer between these two groups, helping facilitate places and opportunities where the rich and the poor can develop mutually beneficial relationships for the good of all. This is true redistribution of wealth.

THE RELATIONAL WAY

At the center of God's Kingdom are relationships. Relationships are the focus of His plan for accomplishing His purposes on earth. One of the greatest downfalls of the modern church era is the movement away from genuine relationships and into the corporate model of the church where we think the most important thing is to increase our market share and expand our influence through size, numbers, and a year-over-year increase in attendance and giving. I would not be too surprised to see the day when a church has an IPO and begins selling private stock to investors.

Robert Farrar Capon says it best when he concludes his analysis of the corporate church model by saying this: "The corporate model is, hands down, the worst thing that ever happened to the church."[18] Yet we have adopted the corporate model because we think big churches can do everything better. We feel that big problems require big answers and big bank accounts to offer big solutions. And to get the big bank accounts, we need big donors, so we can pool lots of money to make the biggest difference in a big world of big needs.

But as more and more churches are beginning to understand, this "big is better" approach does not work. At least, it does not work when you are attempting God's way of doing things. While it maybe be true that large pools of institutional money are better at buying political favors, influencing scientific research, and swaying foreign governments, it has always been known and is frequently demonstrated that individuals always do better at loving and caring for other individuals, tend to be wiser stewards of money, and view their giving and ser-

---

[18] Robert Farrar Capon, *The Astonished Heart: Reclaiming the Good News From the Lost-and-Found of Church History* (Grand Rapids: Eerdmans, 1996), 93.

vice toward others as a means of actually helping them, rather than a means to gain political power or popular prestige.

So when there is a vast need which affects millions of people, there are only two choices. First, an organization can be formed which raises millions of dollars and throws money at the faceless masses, hoping against hope that some of it "sticks" and a few people are helped. The second option is that millions of people can go out and develop loving relationships with the millions of people in need, so that love and service is partnered with financial assistance and education.

In the first instance, all that is usually accomplished is the mass of needy people become a mass of dependent people. Nothing really changes in their lifestyle or outlook. Millions of dollars cannot be managed properly to meet individual needs, or to provide any long term solutions. While some are undoubtedly helped, there is also vast amount of waste, fraud, abuse, and people slipping through the cracks with this approach.

In the second instance, where individual relationships are developed in the process of helping individual needs, the mass of needy people are transformed through loving personal relationships in which they are coached and trained to make any necessary changes in their life. Maybe they are just provided with the means, resources, and personal accountability to climb up to the next step. In return, the people who serve and help others are blessed themselves. They gain a sense of satisfaction, significance, and joy because they are doing something more with their lives than sign their name on a check.

I would like to see ministries and non-profit organizations rise up where the call is no longer, "Send us your money so we can give it to the poor" but rather, "Come with us to develop long-term relationship with the poor (or whoever), so that over time you can meet their needs personally."

People with needs don't always need money. They need love. They need relationships. They need care, protection, and guidance. Yes, financial assistance may be part of this from time to time, but money will not be the answer for everything.

If you have money you want to use to help others in need, you would be better off (as would the people who need the help) to put it to use in your own town, your own neighborhood, and your own city. Don't just write a check. Go down and actually sit with the people you are feeding. Serve them. Talk to them. Hang out with them. Love them. Be with them. This is incarnational living. This is being Jesus to the world. This is loving others like Jesus.

If you think needy people do not exist in your community, your probably are not looking hard enough. Begin by praying for God to show you who they are and where they live and work, and then, pray for the courage and wisdom on how to do more than just put some money in a plate or write a check to an organization.[19] You may pass on the offering plate, but don't pass to the other side of the road when you see a fellow person in need.

Frequently, we send money to churches and ministry organizations because we don't know that there are other options, and we don't know what we can possibly do in our own communities. So while there is no way we could possibly cover all the options for you to love and serve others in your community, let me suggest a few ideas and resources which will help you start building relationships and loving others in tangible ways in your own community.

First and foremost, caring for others needs to be natural and relational. It needs to be something that flows out of relationships that being developed. We should never go to someone we barely know with the intention of fixing their needs, just so we

---

[19] There are numerous websites out there that could be helpful for you in finding others in need. See below for some suggestions.

can go on to someone else who has needs. No, the
of a long-term relationship and friendship mus
foremost in our goals.

If all we are going to do is show up in a home
dump a bunch of food on the sidewalk, and shout,
you!" and then get out of there as quickly as we ca
to our comfortable living rooms and well-stocked
we are missing the point of helping others. The de
a long-term relationship is the primary goal.

Once we have these relationships, or are in th
developing them, it is then that we can begin to lo
to love and serve the others within these various r
And when it comes to this, it is impossible to g
instructions, for the variety of ways you can lov
others are as diverse and numerous as there are
people on earth.

Nevertheless, some examples of what others are
been helpful for me in this area, and I want to shar
some of the books and resources which I have found
ful. At the top of the list are some blog posts by San
GraceGround.com. He has written a helpful and ins
ries of blogs posts on "Getting to Know Your Neighl
another series on "Being the Church in the Con
which are full of practical suggestions on developin
ships with people in your neighborhood, and looking
ble ways to love and serve them. I cannot recomm
blog posts enough.

Second, Josh Reeves is planting a church in Rou
Texas, and he recently wrote a list of 100 ways to en
neighborhood.[22] Many of these are similar to the sorts

---

[20] http://www.graceground.com/community/getting-to-know-your-neighl

[21] http://www.graceground.com/community/being-the-church-in-the-com

[22] http://dl.dropbox.com/u/7105292/Posted%20Resources/100%20Ways
Engage%20Your%20Neigbhorhood.pdf

am Riviera suggested in his posts. The idea, of course, is not just to do one of these, and then dump the gospel message on them, but to host many of these so that you develop ongoing relationships with people in your neighborhood, and over time, learn better how to love and serve them. Some of these activities can get expensive, but when you consider such expenses to be your "tithe" then they no longer become an expense, but simply another way of serving God and others with your time and money.

Third, there are two books which I have found to be helpful as well in giving ideas on how to serve others. These two books are *101 Ways to Reach Your Community* by Steve Sjogren, and *101 Ways to Help People in Need* by Steve and Janie Sjogren.[23] Several of the suggestions in each book might be a little too "churchy" for some of us, and most of the suggestions seem to involve creative ways of inviting people to attend your church, such as pasting church business cards to the backs of dollars bills and then randomly "tipping" people. But if you get rid of the gimmicky aspects of these ideas, many of them would work quite well in an ongoing effort to develop relationships and friendships with certain people in the neighborhood.

Finally, I recently learned of a website called The Relational Tithe where people with skills and a willingness to serve can be linked together with others who have needs.[24] The site is fairly new and I am not sure how well it will work, but I joined the site and will see what comes of it. I am hopeful that it will provide a way for people who want to serve with people who are truly in need.

Ultimately, "giving your money to God" is not about putting some in an offering plate on Sunday morning, or writing a

---

[23] Steve Sjogren, *101 Ways to Help People in Need* (Colorado Springs: NavPress, 2002); Steve Sjogren, *101 Ways to Reach Your Community* (Colorado Springs: NavPress, 2001).
[24] https://www.relationaltithe.com/index.php

check to your favorite charity. While you can do this with some of your money, the truly biblical model of giving money to God is making your finances available for the work of the kingdom in your own neighborhood and community, among the people with whom you live and work. This way of giving is more meaningful for you, more meaningful for them, and helps you put the love of Jesus and the values of the Kingdom of God into action in a tangible way with the people whom God has placed in your life.

Being the church in the community is not about dropping some bucks in the plate on Sunday morning, or even about giving some bucks from your wallet to the guy on the street as you hurry by on your way to work. Yes, money may be involved, but truly being the church in the community is about building relationships with others and loving people where they are at, doing what you can to be a blessing to them, and allowing them to bless you in their own way.

3

SELL YOUR BUILDING

---

*[Jesus'] attitude toward the Temple was not
"this institution needs reforming," nor "the
wrong people are running this place," nor yet
"piety can function elsewhere too." His
deepest belief regarding the Temple was
eschatological: the time had come for God to
judge the entire institution. —N. T. Wright*

Unless you've been under a rock for the past twenty years,
you have probably heard at least one sermon or read one article
or book about how the church is not a building. Generally, the
exhortation is to stop *going* to church, and start *being* the
church. Of course, most of those who say this don't actually
mean that Christians should stop meeting together or going to a
particular building at a certain time to perform various religious
activities. What they mean is that we should not think of the
place we meet as "church." Instead, we should start thinking of
the church as the people who meet.

While I certainly agree with this idea, I am not sure that it will ever catch on, especially when "attending church" continues to be the emphasis in many churches. Pastors and other church leaders are forever encouraging people to attend church *more often* as a sign of true commitment to Jesus, and if you have ever gone through evangelism training you know that it is often stressed that new converts be told about the importance of attending church. It doesn't matter if we are talking about a mega church or house church, this is often the emphasis. I often find it ironic that house churches pride themselves in focusing on the *people* as the church rather than the building, but their very name mentions the *building* where they meet—the house. So almost without exception, the building, despite the language that people use, the *place* that people meet is equated with church. Most people believe that when you are not in the building, you are not in church. People pay lip service to the idea of church as the people of God, but in practice, most do not believe a person is truly part of the church unless they are sitting in a building called "church" at least several times a month.

WHEREVER YOU GO, THERE YOU ARE

As I have argued in my book, *Skeleton Church*, church is the people of God who follow Jesus into the world. This is true whether they meet in a building or not. As the people of God, there can be only one church, the universal church (not to be confused with the Universalist Church), and all believers in Jesus Christ throughout time are part of this church. We are one body, united by one Spirit. Therefore, logically and biblically, wherever you are, there is the church. In other words, you do not go to church; the church goes with you.

Right before GPS units became widely available, my father purchased a Palm Pilot. Remember those? This was before the days of smart phones, and the Palm Pilot functioned as a handheld organizer and nothing else. One day he said he wanted to show me the new GPS program he had downloaded for free from the internet. He handed me his Palm Pilot, and on the screen was a big "X." Underneath the "X" were the words, "You are here."

I laughed, but I have always thought about this when people ask me where I go to church. Whenever I get this question, I often tell them "Right here." After a bewildered look around, they often ask what I mean, and we have a great conversation about following Jesus, and how we do not *go* to church because we *are* the church. I do not *go* to church; the church *goes* with me just as the church goes with you.

TWO OR THREE

The primary objection to this view of church is that you can't have church by yourself. Matthew 18:19-20 is often brought up, which says that wherever two or three are gathered together in the name of Jesus, He is there with them in their midst.

But this is one of those verses (like every other verse in the Bible) where context is key. In the immediately preceding passage, Jesus is providing instructions on how to restore a fellow Christian who is sinning to the community. It is after these instructions that Jesus talks about two or three gathering in His name. So what Jesus is saying is that when the church is trying to restore a sinning brother, He is there with them, helping them make wise and loving decisions for the good of the sinning brother and the entire church as a whole. The verse has nothing to do with determining what is church and what isn't, but everything to do with how the church can help one of its straying members.

Even without the context to guide us, however, a little theological reflection shows that Matthew 18:19-20 cannot be used to define a church meeting. If Jesus is saying that He is only present when two or three are gathered, does this mean that Jesus is not present with each one of us as we go about our day? Is He not with you when you pray, when you go to work, and when you face trials and temptations? Is Jesus not with the Chinese pastor in a solitary confinement prison cell? Is He not with the single mother as she struggles to raise her children by herself?

To ask such questions is to answer them. The rest of Scripture makes clear that we are in Christ and He is in us, and He will never leave us nor forsake us, and no matter where we go or what we do, He is right there also. It might be more precise to say that we go with Him, but that's a subject that was also covered in *Skeleton Church*.

Someone might object, of course, "Of course Jesus is with individual believers wherever they go, but no one can be the church alone. Church requires community." Right. I have never said otherwise. Though Matthew 18:19-20 does not define church as wherever two or three are gathered, it is nevertheless true that you cannot be the church by yourself.

NO GOING ROGUE

As we seek to be the church, we cannot go rogue. Isolation from other believers is never wise, and is actually quite dangerous. Though you are still "in church" even when you are not physically with other believers, this does not mean that we should avoid gathering together with other believers. You and I cannot function as the church when we live as Lone Ranger Christians. While the church is with you wherever you go, the church is not "just Jesus and me." All believers around the world and throughout time are the church, and in order to function as the church we must seek opportunities to gather together with one another.

These gatherings with others can be at a structured time and place, but they need not be. When we seek to live in community with others as part of the Body of Christ, the key word is "live." Church happens as life happens. We are the church with one another as we seek to simply live our life among and with others, loving them as Jesus loved, serving them as Jesus served, and being with them as Jesus is with us. If you want to know how to be the church in your community, it is as simple as living life with a view toward loving others. Again, I have covered this in some detail in my book *Put Service Back into the Church Service*, and so will not discuss it in more detail here.

THE VIEW FROM THE STREET

So what does all this have to do with buildings? The answer is: Nothing. The church has nothing to do with buildings. Though buildings may be used by the church, buildings are not required to be the church. Buildings may help the church accomplish its mission, but at the same time, the church must admit that buildings may often hinder the mission of the church as well. One thing the church must not do, however, is treat buildings like holy sacred places where the truly spiritual stuff happens and everywhere else as secular and unspiritual. Nothing could be further from the truth.

Yet it is exactly this untruth which pervades the thinking of vast majority of people in our world today, both Christian and non-Christian alike. And who can blame them? On the side of almost every building where the church gathers is the word "Church." Even during the times of the week when nobody is in that building, the word is still there. The word is on reader boards in the front lawn, and as people drive to work they see billboard signs with pictures of a building and an invitation to "Come to church." If they do "come to church" one of the first things they hear upon entering the building is someone saying, "Welcome to church." The clear message is that you aren't in church until you walk through those front doors. It is no wonder that when people think of church, they think of buildings.

On top of all this, we treat church buildings unlike any other building. It gets special decorations, special music, special art, and most of all, special behavior. When you are in this building, you must wear certain clothes, say (or not say) certain things, and act in certain ways. It is "in church" that we talk in hushed voices, sing songs of subdued worship, and bow our heads politely in prayer. Unless of course you are in a more contemporary church, in which case, it is "in church" that you shout pious words you would never shout anywhere else, wave your arms about wildly, and tell people constantly that you are experiencing the joy of the Lord when you are actually feeling nothing of the sort.

It is "in church" that we put on our Christian best, including the Christian smile and the Christian hand-shake, while carrying the Christian Bible and trying to think only Christian thoughts. Even the most liberal and modern churches still have a different code of ethics and behavior that one must follow when a person is "in church." If you go outside these often unwritten boundaries, someone pulls you aside (or calls you out from the pulpit) and tells you that such things are inappropriate for "God's House."

Furthermore, when the building is equated with "church," people often compartmentalize their lives so that God is kept safely locked away in the building during the week until they return next Sunday. Church buildings allow us to think that what we do on Sunday morning in that building is "God's domain" and what we do the rest of the week is "real life." Worship becomes something we do at church, rather than a way of life. In this way, buildings tend to get in the way of following Jesus and worshipping God because we have trouble seeing that following Jesus and worshipping God can be done just as well outside of a building as in one. When buildings are equated with church, we have trouble seeing past the building for how we can be the church.

Though these sorts of problems with church buildings are not quite as prevalent in house churches, they can still be found. No matter what goes on in the house during the week, it seems that when "church is happening" the household rules change. When the guitar comes out and the hands go up, the house is magically transformed into a place with a dress code, new rules for behavior, and God-approved language. I've even seen house churches where "during the service" children are shushed, and not allowed to run and play. The buildings of many house churches still function the same as buildings of mega churches, only on a much smaller scale.

If all of this is not the church is supposed to be, how is it that this became the primary mode of "doing church"? How did all of this happen? How did we get here? How did the place where believers meet for mutual edification and encouragement become equated with "the church" itself?

CONSTRUCTION DECONSTRUCTION

A full-length book is needed to fully explain the cultural and theological history about how the church began to identify itself with a building.[25] Let me try to summarize this history in a few paragraphs.

First, it is crucial to remember that almost all of the first followers of Jesus were Jewish. There were a few Samaritans (cf. John 4) and an isolated Gentile or two (Matt 8:5-10; 15:21-28),

---

[25] For information on the history of church buildings, see Jacques Ellul, *The Subversion of Christianity* (Grand Rapids: Eerdmans, 1986), 19-51; Frank Viola and George Barna, *Pagan Christianity? Exploring the Roots of our Christian Practices* (Carol Stream, IL: Barna, 2008), 9-46.

but for the most part, the masses that followed Jesus were Jewish. Even after the birth of the church in Acts 2, the vast majority of the early Christians were Jewish, and most of the Gentiles who converted were "God fearers" which means that they knew and respected the teachings of Judaism, and in many cases, even followed many of the Jewish traditions and practices (cf. Acts 10:2).

So it is no surprise that when the early church began to meet for encouragement and edification, they followed the pattern with which they were already familiar. They pulled traditions and meeting habits from Judaism. They did not invent "house churches." It is somewhat unlikely they even sat down to think about how they should meet and function, but simply adopted the patterns and structure they already knew from the Synagogue gatherings. Initially, they probably even met in Synagogue buildings until the Jewish leadership kicked them out for believing that Jesus was the Messiah. When this occurred, many of them started synagogues in their own homes, just as it was done in the Jewish homes. All Jewish synagogues began as meetings in homes. As the groups grew to more than ten families or so, they would seek to construct a synagogue building in which they could gather more easily. We can imagine the early church tried to follow this pattern, but as house churches grew, they were not able to construct synagogues of their own because of persecution by the Jews.

As Gentiles were added to the church, they often followed the Jewish traditions, and met in home synagogues as well. Not being Jewish, and due to persecution, they probably did not call their groups "synagogues" (Gk. *sunēgogon,* meaning "to assemble, gather together") and went instead with the related term *"ekklēsia"* ("to assemble, come together") which gets translated as "church." Sometimes, when they outgrew homes, they met other gathering places, such as community educational centers (Acts 19:9). What mattered to them was not where or when they met, but how and why. The purpose was always for teaching, encouragement, and the mutual edification of other believers.

Over the next couple hundred years, the Roman Empire began persecuting Christians. Christians were viewed as bad citizens of Rome because they did not swear loyalty to the Emperor or participate in pagan temple rituals. In a culture where there is no distinction between religion and politics, those who do not follow the religion of the Empire are political threats to the Empire. This is crucial to understanding the importance of what happened in the early fourth century under the rule of three different Emperors.

In 312 AD, as Emperor Constantine was preparing his troops for the Battle at Milvian Bridge, he saw a vision in the sky of a cross of light and the words, "In this sign, conquer!" So he had all the soldiers paint a Christian symbol (the Greek *Chi-Rho*) on their shields, and in the ensuing battle, they soundly defeated their enemy. Believing that Jesus had led him to a great victory and had blessed his reign over the Roman Empire, Constantine had himself baptized as a Christian and in 313 AD, issued the Edict of Milan which essentially ceased all persecution against Christians and named himself as the patron of Christianity. In this way, Christianity became a "legal" religion in the Empire. Millions of people converted, not so much because they had become convinced of the truth of Christianity, but because they wanted to be on the same "side" as the Emperor.

However, about fifty years later, in 363 AD, Emperor Julian tried to stop the tide of people turning to Christianity. He himself converted from Christianity back to Paganism, and wrote a short book called *Against the Galileans*, in which he condemned followers of Jesus as delusional, slovenly heretics. He accused them of welcoming anybody into their meetings, even sinners, and of adopting only the worst parts of Judaism and Paganism, but none of the good parts. On this, he writes:

> I wished to show that the Jews agree with the Gentiles, except that they believe in only one God. That is indeed peculiar to them and strange to us; since all the rest we have in common with them—temples, sanctuaries, altars, purifications, and certain precepts. For as to these we differ from one another either not at all or in trivial matters ...

By this, we see that so far, the church had not yet adopted the use of temples, sanctuaries, rites, and other ceremonies that the Pagan religions had in common with Judaism. However, they had started to use the power they had gained under Constantine to mistreat people of other religions the way they themselves had been mistreated. Julian describes the behavior of some Christians this way:

> You emulate the rages and bitterness of the Jews, overturning temples and altars, and you slaughtered not only those of us who remained true to the teachings of their fathers, but also men who were as much astray as yourselves, heretics, because they did not wail over the corpse in the same fashion as yourselves. But these are rather your own doings; for nowhere did either Jesus or Paul hand down to you such commands. The reason for this is that they never even hoped that you would one day attain to such power as you have.

The transition from humility and service to power and authority was taking place. That which Jesus rejected in the wilderness temptation was being adopted by the church.

Emperor Julian was not successful in stamping out Christianity and returning the Roman Empire to Paganism, and in 380 AD, Emperor Theodosius declared all other religions false, and

Christianity to be the *only* approved religion of the Roman Empire. While most believed this to be a huge victory for the cause of Christ, some people have wondered whether it might not have been our greatest defeat.

In a culture where there was no distinction between religion and politics, a declaration that Christianity is the only approved religion had far-reaching effects. People as far away as Germania (Germany) and Britannia (Great Britain), who knew next to nothing about Christianity, were told that the Empire was now Christian, and it would be prudent for them to convert.

But how does one convert to another religion when nothing is known about the religion you are converting to? The answer is simple: you change what you call yourself, but go on doing what you have always done. You continue the feasts, festivals, rites, and ceremonies that you and your ancestors have always practiced, but you now call them "Christian" feasts, festivals, ceremonies, and rites. After all, it was not like anybody around could tell you that you were doing it wrong. They didn't know anything about Christianity either! Priests of other religions continued to be priests, but they were now Christian priests. Pagan holidays continued to be practiced and observed, but they were adopted and adapted by Christianity and given new meaning and interpretations that fit better with Christian theology and ideas.

One of the most influential additions to Christianity was the mass inclusion of thousands of temples across the entire Roman Empire into Christian ownership and Christian practice. Temples and shrines that had previously been used as part of the Emperor cult now became Christian temples. However, other than what deity the prayers were said to, little else changed in these buildings as far as decorations and service structure. Though some of these temples and shrines were torn down and destroyed, most remained intact. It was thought that destroying or abandoning the buildings would be unwise and unproductive. Besides, the new religion of the Empire needed somewhere to teach and train all the new converts about their new faith. The temples, it was argued, could be used to serve that purpose well.

There were, of course, numerous Christian voices that sounded the alarm about all the ideas and practices being adopted into Christianity by the ignorant masses. Several of these leaders developed an approved set of doctrines and teachings which should be taught to all the new "converts" in all the new temples owned by the church, and they quickly developed a system to send out a small army of teachers and priests to distribute these Empire-approved church doctrines.

To defend and explain many of these developments, newly empowered church leaders also developed a theological defense for the priesthood, the hierarchy, the power, the money, and the buildings. Their argument rested primarily on the idea that the Kingdom of God had overtaken the kingdoms of the world, and the riches and power of the worldly kingdoms were now being used to help expand the Kingdom of God even further upon the earth.

The defense of church buildings consisted largely of looking back to the temple of the Jews in Jerusalem, and to the future rule and reign of Jesus Christ on earth. It was argued that since God allowed Solomon to build a grand and glorious temple where the Jews could worship Him, it was necessary for Christians to worship God in a similar fashion. Many in the church argued further that the conversion of the pagan temples brought the world one step closer to the ultimate goal of spreading Christianity throughout the entire earth. Other pagan nations would become Christian nations and pagan rulers would become Christian rulers, just as had happened to the Roman Empire.

It was thought that eventually the entire world would become Christian, thus ushering in the return of Jesus and the eternal kingdom. Once a few more regions had been converted to Christianity (by the sword if necessary), Jesus would return and rule the earth in peace and prosperity for all. The money and the power of the church, represented in large part by the buildings, were viewed as both the means and the signs that God's Kingdom was advancing upon the earth.

MEGA CHURCH MULTIPLICATION

Not much has changed in the last 1700 years. We still construct our temples and buildings and equate them with evidence that God is working in and through the church. If the numbers of buildings keep increasing, and the new buildings that go up are larger and grander than any built before, God must be blessing the work. And so pastors build Crystal Cathedrals and convert former basketball coliseums into church buildings. To compete, older churches spend as much as $150 million to renovate and update their downtown building. In some places of our country, you can drive for a mile, and see one mega church after another lined up along the road, competing with each other for parking space and people. All of this is taken as a sign that God is pleased and that Christianity is advancing in the world.

It is no good looking wistfully at the past, wishing something different had been done. In all likelihood, if we had been alive back in the days of Constantine, none of us would have done anything different. After all, what else could be done?

So although we cannot unmake the decisions of the church in the past, we can make our own decisions today. There are a growing number of Christians worldwide who do not think the best way to carry forward the Kingdom of God is by emulating Super Bowls with roaring crowds, rock concerts with strobe lights and fog machines, or Wheel-of-Fortune game-show giveaways. Though there is nothing wrong with these cultural activities, nor is there anything sinful with Christians participating in them, it could be argued that they simply do not reflect the quiet, self-sacrificing, mission-oriented service of Jesus, or what He wants for those who follow Him. While there are times where such showy activities might be appropriate for followers of Jesus, it seems that most of the time, these activities are more in line with the promises of power, greed, and popularity that Satan offered to Jesus in the wilderness temptations, and could probably be avoided without doing any damage whatsoever to the work of God in the world. We can know this because of the way Jesus Himself lived during His ministry, and especially in light of how He viewed the religious buildings of His day, and specifically, the Jewish temple.

JESUS HAS LEFT THE BUILDING

In the days of Jesus, the Jewish people believed in a form of incarnation. They did not believe that God could become a man, but that heaven and earth connected at the temple in Jerusalem. God, for the Jewish person, dwelled in some sense in the temple. The temple was seen as the central incarnational symbol of Jewish life.

This is one of the primary reasons that the teachings and actions of Jesus were so controversial. In many different ways and at many different times, Jesus indicated that He was the new temple; that in Him people could receive forgiveness from sins, access to God, and restoration from exile. So in a time when people believed that God resided in the temple, imagine the shock they would have felt when Jesus announced that the temple would be destroyed (John 2:19-21). This would be like saying that God was not going to protect His house and was abandoning His people.

But as shocking as it was to predict the destruction of the temple in Jerusalem, John indicates that Jesus was actually talking about His own body. Though we tend to think that this would soften the blow of such words for Jewish people at the time, the opposite is actually true.

It was bad enough for Jesus to say that the temple would be destroyed. This was a blasphemous and scandalous teaching for most Jews. But when He claimed that He was replacing the temple and that in Him the temple would be destroyed, this was much worse than simply saying that the temple building itself would be demolished. Why? Because He was claiming to replace the temple, which in the minds of Jews, would be like claiming to replace God. But more than that, if He was replacing the temple and then He Himself was going to be destroyed, there would be no way to rebuild such a temple. The temple as a building could be rebuilt, as it already had been. But if the temple is replaced by a man, and then the man dies, the man cannot be rebuilt, and therefore, the connection between God and man would no longer exist. If there was no temple—either in a building or in a man—then there was no connection between heaven and earth. Where then could a person go who wanted to meet with God? Where then could a person offer their sacrifices and say their prayers? Where then could they get forgiveness and cleansing from sin?

All of this was solved in the resurrection of Jesus from the dead, but became an issue again when Jesus returned to heaven, only to be solved once again at the birth of the church in Acts 2 when the Holy Spirit came upon the believers. Whereas the temple had been replaced by Jesus as the nexus between heaven and earth, the church now "replaced" Jesus. That is, the church *became* Jesus on earth. While as a man, Jesus could only be in one place at one time. As the Head of the church, however, Jesus can be wherever there are members of His body, the church. Just as Jesus was the incarnation of God, so the church is the incarnation of Jesus. We are, therefore, as Paul writes in 1 Corinthians 3:16, the temple of God. We are now the meeting place between heaven and earth. We are the church, the incarnation, the temple of God, the body of Christ to the world.

And yet what have we done since the discovery of this seismic shift in how God relates to mankind? We have gone back to what Jesus so carefully and completely obliterated. We have ignored His work on the cross, His death and resurrection, and the coming of the Spirit at Pentecost, and have returned to constructing our temples as the meeting place between God and man on earth. We refer to these buildings as "God's House" as the place where we go to "meet and worship God." Such ideas deny nearly everything Jesus accomplished and taught! Jesus lived, taught, and died to show the world that God does not dwell in buildings built by human hands. God lives and works and redeems in and through His people, the church. Temple worship could not be reformed; it could only be done away with. Though Jesus said, "Tear down this building. You don't need it. God isn't there anyway. If you remove it, you'll be able to see God so much better," we have responded by constructing even more buildings.

Jesus condemned religious buildings in His day. He prophesied their end, and He refocused the worship of God in Himself. He killed the building. But we resurrected the building. It's been 2000 years, and we still believe that God is most active in and through a building. Yet if Jesus has left the building, and destroyed it on His way out, we must think carefully before embarking on our own building campaigns. We erect church buildings at great cost and loss because we are trying to construct a building that has been condemned.

CONDEMNED BUILDINGS

Many believe there is no harm in church buildings. In fact, most believe that there is more harm in *not* having a building than having one because of how they provide convenience for gathering, a social identity for the people, and a position of prominence in the community. While it could easily be argued that these are not truly beneficial, but detrimental, to our place in the world, there are two main problems with church buildings and how they hinder the church's mission. Like Hiel trying to rebuild Jericho in 1 Kings 16:34, we lay the foundation at the cost of our firstborn son, and erect the gates at the cost of our youngest. But in our cast, our oldest son is our finances and our youngest son is our mission.

First, buildings bind the church with financial burdens. The biggest two expenses in most church budges are pastoral salaries and mortgage payments. Imagine how much money could be freed up for local and global missions if one (or both) of these budget items disappeared. A gathering of believers must ask themselves if a mortgage payment every month—whether it is $500 or $5,000—could accomplish more if put toward helping the poor and sick in the community. When we saddle our people with huge financial burdens, it vastly limits and restricts who and how we love and serve others in the surrounding community.

Second, buildings blind the church to the idea that mission can take place outside of the building. Many churches that own buildings seek to justify the cost of the building by holding every possible meeting and outreach within the building. If the church decides to feed the hungry, they cook the meal in the church kitchen, set tables in the church dining hall, and invite the poor and the hungry to come to the church for a free meal. While feeding the hungry is not bad, it is not best done inside the four walls of a church building. And this is just one example. Look at any church calendar, and you will see that most of the weekly and monthly activities that are done within the four walls of the church building, could also be done out in the community—and probably with greater impact.

131

For these reasons, the church building must be condemned. The construction of a building must no longer be the default position in local churches, where those who do not want to build must defend their position to those who do. Rather, the default position among local churches should not be to spare no expense in their construction, but to avoid church buildings at all costs. A building might be necessary in some extreme cases, but construction should commence only after careful consideration of the missional and theological ramifications for what that building will do to the life, health, and mission of the church.

THE CHURCH OF BUILDINGS

Every time I enter a building where a church meets, I am reminded of something one of my seminary professors said: "First we make our buildings; then our buildings make us." It seems that far too often, a church is formed and influenced more by its buildings than by Scripture or even by Jesus Christ. We defend our buildings and what we do in them more than we defend the fatherless, the widows, the poor, the hungry, and the destitute. Sometimes we defend our buildings more than the gospel itself.

Many years ago when I was just beginning to come to grips with much of what I now believe about church, I thought that I still wanted to be a pastor. In one of the church I applied for, they told me some about their history and how they had started as a home Bible study, and eventually grew to be a church of about 400, with Sunday morning and Sunday night services, a vibrant youth group, a growing children's ministry, and a building that was completely paid for.

As we talked, I praised them for the work they were doing in their community and asked the elders who were interviewing me what they would do if they all felt that God was calling them to sell their building so that they could do even more and better ministry in the community. I thought it was an easy answer, but much to my surprise, they unanimous agreed that God would never call them to do this because they needed their building to do the ministry God had called them to do. They could not imagine doing church ministry without a church building, and so assumed that God would never ask them to sell their building, even if it meant greater and more effective ministry. While not every church would respond similarly, I think that such an attitude is more prevalent than we want to believe.

A church that might begin in simplicity, with fellowship and service being the focus of their community, radically changes once it constructs a building. It now becomes focused on filling the pews, upgrading the sound system, paving the parking lot, and paying the mortgage. Whereas before the church used to go into the community and get involved in their events, now the church invites the community into the church building to attend the church events. Churches that used to perform ministry in the community quite well before they had a building, suddenly find that a building is indispensable for ministry once they obtain one.

All of this leads me to believe that we are no longer the church of Jesus; we are the church of buildings. We strive for buildings and work for our buildings. We live and die for our buildings. We protect them at all cost. We defend them to the death. We are jealous of the buildings of bigger churches and newer churches. We fight for our right to own buildings, keep buildings, and meet in buildings. Yet as Howard Snyder pointed out in his 1975 message at the Lausanne Conference on Evangelism: "In many Western cities, the last thing the church needs is more buildings!"[26]

---

[26] Howard A. Snyder, "The Church as God's Agent in Evangelism" in *Let the Earth Hear His Voice*, ed. James Dixon (Minneapolis, World Wide: 1975), 358.

Returning to the mission and message of Jesus might require us to give up our buildings. If you are part of a church that has a building, and you think that possibly you have become too dependent on your building for ministry, let me propose a radical solution: consider selling your church building.

SELL YOUR BUILDING

If your church has more than 20 people, you probably feel that selling your building is not an option. It may be fine for a church of a dozen people to meet in someone's house, but that is unrealistic for a church of 50 or 100, let alone a church of 1000 or more.

But if a church really wants to escape the pitfalls of power and control that come with buildings, there are only two options: you must either sell the building or find another way to break free of the issues and pitfalls of owning a building. In this section, we will look at how your church could still function if you decide to sell your building. In a later section, we will survey some suggestions for redeeming your building if you decide to retain it.

Of course, there is always the possibility that you don't need a building at all. The church can exist quite well without any buildings of any sort. I know this is a radical suggestion, but I invite you to consider the possibility anyway. It is something I propose and defend in my book *Put Service Back into the Church Service.*

But if you want to have a regular place to meet, but want to sell your building for ministry purposes, and still need a place to meet for "Church Services," there are only a few options. No, you will not have to meet in an old circus tent or under a tree somewhere, though if either of those fit your situation, they are not necessarily bad ideas. Remember, Saddleback Community Church started out by meeting in tents, and many

African churches still meet under trees. But these options are not available or possible for most.

There are three realistic options for churches that sell their buildings but still need a place to meet: they need to find a place that is free, find a place to rent, or break up into smaller units. Let us look at each.

1. Find a place that is free. There are many possibilities for free places to meet. Sometimes other churches might let you use their facilities for free, though often not at times you want. Another option might be to use a community center, but many of these also require rental fees. Some churches meet in local parks, on beaches, or in campgrounds. Recently, a coworker of mine told me that he was out hiking in the woods, and stumbled into a church service in the middle of the woods. That sounds a little cultish, but it could be fun.

Occasionally, local bars or coffee houses will allow churches to meet for free, as long as people buy food and beverages. This often works out well since many of these sites already have sound equipment set up. But again, bars are generally not large enough to accommodate too many people, and it is often difficult to do anything with children.

2. Find a place to rent. Though some of the suggestions above may not be free, many of those places are available to rent. In addition, churches might meet in school auditoriums, theaters, hotels, YMCAs, conference rooms, restaurants, and any other place that has an open room. One of the difficulties with these areas, as well as with the free areas, is setting up. If your church has over 50 people, setting up chairs and a sound system every week can get tiresome.

However, it can be done. Rolling Hills Baptist Church in Fayetteville, GA decided that to have more money for outreach and service in the community, they should sell their building. The church has more than 100 people who attend. It owned a building for more than 20 years, and decided to rent another facility in town at about one-third the cost of owning. When interviewed, here is what was reported in the news:

> The church has a new mission. Instead of investing in the property that consumed most of their budget, they will use the more than $1-million dollars from the sale to invest in people who have needs. "It's just a way of looking at this property differently," Pastor Mercer said. "We saw it as an asset we could liquidate and turn around and use that resource to meet the needs of people.[27]

3. Break up into smaller units. The third option is a combination of finding a place that's free and finding a place to rent, and avoids most of the labor-intensive setup and takedown. This option is to become something like a network of cell groups. In this instance, the church decides that it does not have to meet as a large congregation every week, but only needs to meet every six weeks, or once a quarter. On these large gathering days, a place will be rented and set up to accommodate everyone. During the rest of the weeks, the church meets in smaller units of 5-15 people, meeting in free locations of their choice. Some might meet weekly at the beach. Others at Starbucks. Some in homes or parks.

Of the three options above, this third option is probably the best since it allows the church to spread out in the community for the greatest impact, costs little money, and provides a way for the greatest intimacy and fellowship among the members. The only people who may not like it are the pastoral staff who are no longer "up front" every single week.

If you have a church building and are looking for ways to implement one of the ideas above, you may have questions about how to go about selling your building.

---

[27] http://www.11alive.com/news/news_story.aspx?storyid=141948&catid=40

HOW TO SELL YOUR BUILDING

Some feel that selling a church building is a bad investment. But is it? It all depends on the perspective.

When we own buildings, people associate the church with a building rather than with people. If we don't own buildings, people may come to understand the church is not about where we meet or what our building looks like, but is rather the people of God living the gospel within the world. With a building, if we grow we have to move or build an addition. If we shrink, we have sell or declare bankruptcy. Without a building, we are more flexible and free to follow Jesus where He leads.

If you do decide to sell your building, one question you may ask—especially if you have a traditional building with stained glass and a steeple—is, "Who would buy it?" Well, you might be surprised. There are a few organizations and businesses that might be eager to buy a place like yours.

1. Sell to yourself. At the top of the list of organizations that might like to buy your building is your own organization. That's right. You can sell your building to yourself. I don't mean to you personally, as the pastor. (Though I have read of some churches that do this, I do not recommend it. It is a shady practice). No, to sell it to yourself, a few members of the church could start a non-profit organization that is dedicated to helping a certain group of people in the community. As part of helping and loving these people, the newly-formed organization will need a building that can accommodate large gatherings as well as small classes. What better location than a church? Once the organization is formed, the church can sell its building to the organization.

Then, as part of its activity in the community, and to maintain its financial integrity, the organization could rent the building back to the church. Depending on the financial situation of the organization, the building could even be used for free educational or service needs in the community.

Why couldn't a church just do this on their own? They could, and probably should. But the sad fact is that many don't. When it comes to church buildings, most church boards are primarily concerned with maintaining the cleanliness and purity of the church grounds. People with beer cans, cigarette butts, or bad language are typically not allowed on the premises. So for this option to properly work, the board members of the organization must have a clear vision for serving the community, rather than just being a front for the church to continue as usual. If the organization exists just to keep the church running as usual, there is no point to creating an additional link in the chain, and this option should be ignored. If the organization has a clear vision of serving the community, then they should be able to tell the church that the building is now a "Community Building" and there will undoubtedly be groups that meet in the building during the week who have "un-Christian" behavior and habits. But the church should be fine with this, because it is not "their" building any longer. It is simply a community building they are renting for their meeting needs.

2. Sell to another church. There are almost always other churches in town looking to move from renting a school to having their own building. If you are trying to move in the opposite direction, you may not be too eager to sell your building to another church in town.

But remember, other churches are not the competition, but are simply on a different path in following Jesus. We are not to judge other servants, but are only to obey the instructions from our own Master. If another church wants to buy a building, and you want to sell one, and both of you believe this will help accomplish your mission in the world, then make the sale. It doesn't matter if they hold a different position on spiritual gifts, women in ministry, or whether or not creation took seven days or seven billion years. We are all part of the same family, and whoever is not against Jesus is for Him. You have a building to sell. They want to buy a building. It's a perfect fit.

Oh, and if you do sell your building to another church, give them a really good price. Maybe you could even just give it to them, or let them take over the mortgage. That would fulfill all sorts of kingdom principles.

On a related note, two or more churches could also consolidate. It is always sad to see two or three churches in the same neighborhood, each with a building that could sit a hundred people or more, but only averaging 35 in weekend attendance. If two or three of these churches consolidated their buildings (and staff), a lot of money could be saved on mortgage payments, with the extra funds going toward meeting needs in the community.

3. Sell it to a business. Sometimes local businesses are eager to get church property because it often has good parking and a central location. If you do sell your building to a business, they will often convert the building into office space, a warehouse, or a training center. I heard of one business that likes to buy up old church buildings and convert them into dance clubs. For some reason, people like to dance in churches. I know that many elders and churchgoers don't like the idea of their building becoming an office complex or dance club, but from God's perspective, is the building really accomplishing its purpose by sitting empty six days of the week, or being a place that Christians dump thousands and millions of dollars into every year just so they can have a place to talk about the Bible? Is that really better? What is a building anyway but a bunch of wood, rock, and metal? There's nothing sacred about it, other than what is sacred about every other building. Just because a secular business or a dance club takes over where a church used to meet does not mean the church is losing ground to the world. To the contrary, if the church has abandoned the building to go serve others in the world, the church has not lost, but has won a victory. If the building *as it is* hinders your mission, and not having a building helps accomplish your mission, dump it as fast as possible to the first buyer and consider the sale an advancement of the Kingdom of God.

I recently read about a church in Albany, New York that sold their building to a Fraternity. The church actually did not want to sell to a Fraternity because of all the drinking and sex that generally goes on in Fraternities. The church members didn't think that such things should happen in a former church building. But eventually, with no other buyers and the bank threatening to foreclose, the church was forced to sell. The Fraternity came in, cleaned up the church, and immediately transformed it, not into a drunken party zone, but into a community center for the neighborhood. They also created a $50,000 fund to provide micro-loans for the community. They brought in soda fountains, coffee makers, pool tables, and other fun activities for families, teenagers, and college students to play. The fraternity transformed an old, dying church into a place for people to hang out, have fun, and get help. Maybe the church would not have died if they had done something similar.

4. Sell to a homeowner. Though most people would not think a church would make a good house, some of the older churches have a lot of style and historical character which is what some homeowners are looking for. A couple in Kyloe, Northumberland, PA bought and converted a church into a home, with the end result being a stunning home. You can probably find pictures of it online.[28]

Yes, some of the suggestions above may seem extreme. But maybe what really is extreme is spending millions of dollars for the construction and upkeep of a building that only gets

---

[28]   http://www.travelet.com/2009/07/one-pair-bought-and-converted-church-into-home-in-kyloe-northumberland/ Here is a another example: http://www.ibtimes.com/articles/89602/20101207/holy-home-stunning-looking-church-for-sale-in-utrecht.htm

used for a few hours a week. Furthermore, these "extreme" suggestions are reality for many of our brothers and sisters throughout time and around the world where their government made it illegal for them to own buildings or meet in large groups. If they can effectively function as the church without buildings, why can't we?

REDEEMING YOUR BUILDING

Maybe you are not convinced. Maybe you cannot imagine doing church without owning a building. Maybe you truly do need to own a building to carry out your God-given mission in your community. There are many churches around the world that own buildings and use them for the Kingdom to the glory of God. Maybe yours is one of them and selling your building might actually interfere with your mission in the world.

Fine.

I am not against buildings *per se*. While I do not believe that church buildings are necessary for most churches to carry out their mission, I also do not believe that owning a church building is necessarily sinful or wrong. Buildings are a tool, and can either help or hinder the mission of the church. There are many cases where buildings can be used effectively.

My primary concern is that for many churches, buildings are chains that hold the people back from truly ministering in an effective way in the community. With buildings come footholds of power, money, and control that hold many congregations back. So to help make sure that the mission of God remains the primary focus in your church, let me suggest three ways that help churches redeem their buildings and protect themselves from many of the pitfalls that come with church structures.

1. Revoke Your Tax-Exempt Status. In the United States, churches do not have to pay property taxes. This is a great benefit to churches, especially when budgets are tight. But have you ever wondered why churches are given tax-exempt status? It has nothing to do with the separation of church and state. The reason churches are given tax-exempt status is the same reason that any other non-profit organization (whether religious or not) is given the same status: they engage in charitable work that benefits the community. The government wants to encourage people to be charitable, and so gives tax-exempt status to charitable organizations.

Therefore, if a church is not engaging in charitable service in the community, it is reasonable to ask them to surrender their tax-exempt status. Churches, like any charitable organization, should only get tax-exempt status if they can show where and how they are providing a service to the community.

"But," a church might say, "We cannot afford to do much in the community. We are barely paying our bills as it is."

But what would you would tell the government if they stepped in and said "Start serving the community or start paying your taxes"? In such a situation, you would quickly find the resources to start serving your community in a tangible way that helps others.

And how much money should be budgeted for service to the community? The place to start, it seems, might be whatever the church would be paying in taxes if they were not tax-exempt.

So no, I am not really suggesting you revoke your tax-exempt status. You can, if you really want to, but in general, churches are better stewards of money than the government. I believe, however, that churches should *act* as if they did pay taxes, and then take that "tax money" and use it in tangible ways for the good of the community. How much money would this be per year?

The national average for property taxes is about 3%. So if your church and property is worth $500,000, you would "tax" yourself $15,000 per year to pour back into the community.

Imagine what your church could do in the community with $15,000! What needs do people petition the local government for, but which the county coffers cannot afford? Can the church help out? What would the city council say if you showed up with $10,000 to help renovate the school, fix that road, or clean that park? Why don't you go and find out?

If this idea caught on around the country, we could solve many problems not only in our own communities, but around the world. It is estimated that the total value of church buildings and property in the United States is about $500 billion. If churches decided to tax themselves at 3% annually, this would create $15 billion per year that the church could use to help the people of our country and others around the world.

When you listen to politicians argue about whether the country can afford to cut just $4 billion out of the annual United States budget, it become mind boggling to realize that if churches would just tax ourselves, the church could be spending $15 billion per year on community service in our communities and elsewhere.

On a related note, it was reported in 1986 that churches around the country had a total annual income from tithes of over $100 billion. If churches taxed this donation income at a rate similar to the corporate tax rate (averaging about 20%), this could generate an additional $20 billion per year to use for the Kingdom of God.

All of this is simply to point out that the church has lots of money, and we should make careful, wise decisions about how we spend it.

So keep your tax-exempt status, but tax yourself what you would be paying if you were not tax-exempt, and then use that money in all the ways government would use it, but with the love of Jesus added in. In such a way, the world will be turned upside down. This is one way to redeem and keep your church buildings.

2. Allow community groups to use the church for free. I always find it ironic that many of our churches have the word "community" plastered on the side of the building, but few churches actually make the building available to the community. Apparently, the community church is only open to the community of people who attend the services. And when someone inquires about renting the building for a wedding, a funeral, or a support group, we tell them they need to come to church on Sunday, sign release forms, pay a deposit and rental fee, and don't drink, smoke, or swear on the premises.

But if we viewed our building not as "the church" but as a building that the church meets in on an occasional basis, then the conflict of what happens in the building the rest of the week disappears. Let me put it another way. If your church did not have a "church building" you would probably have to rent a school gymnasium, a theater, a hotel conference room, or some other sort of multi-purpose building. In such cases, do you care too much about what happens in those rooms the rest of the week? As long as the room is clean on Sunday morning, do you care that on Friday night in the hotel conference room you rent, there was a wedding party with lots of drinking, loud music, some cursing, and a few people "hooked up" afterwards? No, you don't care because it is not your building. The hotel, or whoever owns the building, can do what they want with that room the rest of the week, and the church that meets there on Sunday morning is not profaned by what went on in the same room on Friday night.

This is how churches should view their own buildings. There is nothing holy or sanctified about the church building, any more than there is anything holy or sanctified about the school gymnasium or hotel conference room.

To help redeem our building in this way, it might be best to fully transform the use and availability of our church building. It might be a good idea to recreate church around the current cultural forms of community. Rather than be a church which has a coffee house, we can become a coffee house that has a church. Rather than be a church that offers Wednesday night aerobics, we can become an aerobic and dance center that has a church.

This is beneficial on multiple levels. For example, when organized this way, the building will not sit empty most of the week, the business helps pay the bills, and the gathering center creates opportunities to make connections with the community.

Churches of this type are popping up all over the country. For example, Life in Deep Ellum is a Cultural Arts and Community Center in Dallas, TX. They have a coffee shop called Mokah, a state-of-the-art music venue for concerts, and an expansive gallery for art exhibits. The building also houses a film company, a graphic design company, and a life-coaching and counseling service. On Sunday, a church meets there too.

The church is not a building, and the building is not a church. In the case of Life in Deep Ellum, the building is owned and managed by a group of people who are part of the church. The building is a community center, and the church, as part of the community, meets in the building. The church is not front and center; the community center is. The church is not the focal point of the building; the coffee shop, art gallery, and music venue are.

Woodland Hills Church in St. Paul, MN has undergone a building renovation specifically to provide a homeless shelter, a second-run movie theater, and a training center to provide a life skill and work readiness training center for people in the community.

Fellowship Bible Church in Colorado Springs recently learned that the city passed a "no camping" ordinance to restrict the number of homeless people who were camping in city parks and vacant lots. So the church started letting people camp out on their property—no strings attached.

Kathy Escobar, a pastor at The Refuge in Denver, recently told me of her vision to start an "Adult Orphanage." The church doesn't own any buildings, but one of the first buildings they would like to purchase is an apartment complex so that they could provide affordable housing to low-income and single-parent households. Residents of this apartment complex might be offered job training, financial counseling, and other such items to help them get back on their feet and find a good paying job.

I could go on and on with examples like this from all around the world. I believe that while such examples were relatively rare 20 years ago, more and more churches are finding ways to use their buildings for more than just church meetings and Bible studies. These buildings can be used to help and serve the people in the community, and in this way, bless and love them. Using our buildings this way redeems the buildings for the benefit of the community.

3. Double your mortgage. The third and final way of helping churches redeem their buildings is by doubling the mortgage. At a time when many churches around the country are defaulting on their current mortgage, this is probably not advice that most churches want to receive. However, this recommendation is not really about past debt, but about future debt and budgeting. Many churches, if they had followed this recommendation, would not find themselves in the debt dilemma they now face.

The recommendation is that whenever a church seeks to spend money, they double the cost. The extra money would then go toward missional work and service in the community and around the world. In essence, this recommendation asks churches to put 50% of their budget toward missions. We discussed this idea previously in the chapter on tithing. Church buildings are usually the biggest expense of a church, but this principle could be applied to anything the church spends money on, from pastoral salaries to office supplies. The end result of this is not really that the budget doubles, but that the budget stays the same, and how the money is spent undergoes careful examination. Some churches already give away 50% of their annual budgets toward missions. I congratulate them, but even these churches might be helped by doubling the cost of items they wish to purchase to help them determine if the purchase is important or not.

Such an approach keeps the church priorities in their proper perspective. It guarantees that missional involvement will always be a top priority. It also helps church boards determine which items are really worth buying. So, for example, if the new stained glass windows, which usually cost $20,000, will now cost $40,000 because an additional $20,000 is required for outreach, evangelism, and missions, are the stained glass windows really worth it? If some of the members of the church want a youth pastor, and they think they can get away with paying him $40,000, are they ready to pull $80,000 out of the budget so that the church can have a youth pastor and $40,000 for missions?

This approach is not really something that most churches can jump into right away. If the church budget is already tight, and the pastoral salary and church mortgage are consuming 90% of the budget, it is impossible to double to the budget right away so that an equal amount of money can go toward missions. But future purchases with that remaining 10% can still be put to this sort of test. Would the church continue to buy those nice, pre-printed bulletins if their cost just doubled? Does the church have to buy a video projector and screen? Does the parking lot have to be repaved?

Asking these sorts of questions will help redeem the building, guaranteeing that it will not consume the missional purpose and goals of the church.

Ultimately, the ideas above for how to use your church building for the Kingdom of God are only suggestions. The issue of the church building is quite complex. Many churches may not be able to follow some of the suggestions in this chapter due to liability issues and damage to the facilities that outside groups cause. While sharing or renting facilities is an option for some churches, in many parts of the country, this ends up being much more expensive and time consuming than simply owning.

The main concern of this chapter is for churches to realize that owning—or even using—a building is not required to be the church. The church is lived out in life together with one another. Followers of Jesus can come together, celebrate, thank God for His gifts, and love each other whether they have a building to do this in or not. We must care for each other, laugh together, weep with one another whether we have tax-exempt status or not. While church can be done in a building that we own or rent, all church community activities can also occur in the places of normal life—our homes, offices, parks, cafes, and streets. Instead of building temples and calling them "the house of God" or "church," we can use those same financial resources to help our neighbors in need, whether they live next door or halfway around the world. It is only then that the church looks and loves like Jesus.

In his day, Kierkegaard viewed church buildings as one of the primary factors that inhibited the health and mission of the church. He wrote this:

Think of a hospital. The patients are dying like flies. The methods are altered in one way and another. It's no use. What does it come from? It comes from the building, the whole building is full of poison. That the patients are registered as dead, one of this disease, and that one of another, is not true; for they are all dead from the poison that is in the building.

So it is in the religious sphere. That the religious situation is lamentable, that religiously men are in a pitiable state, nothing is more certain. So one man thinks that it would help if we got a new hymnal, another a new altar-book, another a musical service, etc., etc.

In vain—for it comes from ... the building ...

Let it collapse, this lumber room, get rid of it, shut all these shops and booths ... And let us again serve God in simplicity, instead of treating him as a fool in magnificent buildings.[29]

---

[29] Søren Kierkegaard, *Attack Upon Christendom* (Boston: Beacon, 1957), 139.

CONCLUSION

I sometimes get criticized for being "down on church" but I hope you can see that nothing could be further from the truth. I love the church and want the church to be everything Jesus wants it to be in this world by doing what Jesus wants us to do. But sometimes, being and doing what Jesus wants requires us to ask some hard questions about what we are currently doing as the church. If there are certain practices we engage in or possession we own which hold us back from spreading the good news about Jesus to all the world, from making disciples, and from expanding the rule and reign of God in our lives and the lives of others, then some changes in how we "do" church are required.

Some of the things today which hold the church back from being and doing what Jesus wants are the very things that often get wrongly included in the definition of church. The church is not about the number of people we evangelize, have on our membership rolls, or can get to show up for a Sunday meeting. Nor is the church defined by the number of dollars that get dropped in the offering plate or the size of our annual budget. And though it is common to think of church as a building where Christians meet, the church has never consisted of brick and mortar, wood and nails, or stone and steel.

The church is the people of God who follow Jesus into the world. It doesn't matter how many follow Jesus in this way, they are still the church. It doesn't matter how much money they have in their pockets or give toward their cause, they are still the church. It doesn't matter whether they own a building or even meet in a building, they are still the church.

Do you want to be the church that follows Jesus? Then tell Him so, and have the courage to follow Him wherever He leads, even if it is away from crowds, away from budgets, and away from buildings. The church is not bodies, bucks, or bricks, and if we are going to follow Jesus into the world, He may ask us to leave some of these things behind.

ABOUT THE AUTHOR

Jeremy Myers is an author of numerous books and a blogger at TillHeComes.org, a popular website about following Jesus into the world. His greatest accomplishment in life, however, is raising three beautiful daughters with his wife, Wendy.

Jeremy is also the founder and owner of Redeeming Press, a publishing company built upon the idea that books should be published based on the ideas they contain, rather than on how many copies they will sell. If you are an author who has been rejected by traditional publishing houses because you are not a popular conference speaker, mega church pastor, or radio personality, consider submitting your book to Redeeming Press for publication. Even if you haven't tried to publish through other companies, we would be thrilled to talk with you about publishing your book.

If you appreciated the content of this book, would you consider recommending it to your friends and leaving a review on Amazon? Thanks!

CONNECT WITH JEREMY MYERS

If you want to read some of my other writings or connect with me through Twitter, Facebook, or one of my other social sites, here are some sites where you can do so. I look forward to meeting you online!

TillHeComes.org
RedeemingPress.com
GraceCommentary.com
Twitter.com/jeremyers1
Facebook.com/jeremy.myers3
Facebook.com/jeremy.myers.author
Google.com/+JeremyMyers
Pinterest.com/jeremyers1
LinkedIn/in/jeremyers1
iTunes Podcast

Put Service Back Into the Church Service

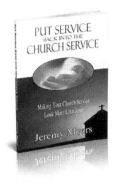

Churches around the world are trying to revitalize their church services. There is almost nothing they will not try. Some embark on multi-million dollar building campaigns while others sell their buildings to plant home churches. Some hire celebrity pastors to attract crowds of people, while others hire no clergy so that there can be open sharing in the service.

Yet despite everything churches have tried, few focus much time, money, or energy on the one thing that churches are supposed to be doing: loving and serving others like Jesus.

Put Service Back into the Church Service challenges readers to follow a few simple principles and put a few ideas into practice which will help churches of all types and sizes make serving others the primary emphasis of a church service.

Reviews from Amazon

Jeremy challenges church addicts, those addicted to an unending parade of church buildings, church services, Bible studies, church programs and more to follow Jesus into our communities, communities filled with lonely, hurting people and BE the church, loving the people in our world with the love of Jesus. Do we need another training program, another seminar, another church building, a remodeled church building, more staff, updated music, or does our world need us, the followers of Jesus, to BE the church in the world? The book is well-written, challenging and a book that really can make a difference not only in our churches, but also and especially in our neighborhoods and communities. –Charles Epworth

Do you ever have an unexplained frustration with your church, its service or programs? Do you ever feel like you are "spinning your wheels" when it comes to reaching others for Christ? This book helps to explain why this might be happening, and presents a convincing argument for why today's church services are mostly ineffective and inefficient. You will read concepts explained that you've not fully heard before. And you will get hints as to how it could, or should, work. –MikeM

Purchase the eBook for $4.99
Purchase the Paperback for $5.99

The Death and Resurrection of the Church

In a day when many are looking for ways to revitalize the church, Jeremy Myers argues that the church should die.

This is not only because of the universal principle that death precedes resurrection, but also because the church has adopted certain Satanic values and goals and the only way to break free from our enslavement to these values is to die.

But death will not be the end of the church, just as death was not the end of Jesus. If the church follows Jesus into death, and even to the hellish places on earth, it is only then that the church will rise again to new life and vibrancy in the Kingdom of God.

Reviews from Amazon

I have often thought on the church and how its acceptance of corporate methods and assimilation of cultural media mores taints its mission but Jeremy Myers eloquently captures in words the true crux of the matter— that the church is not a social club for do-gooders but to disseminate the good news to all the nooks and crannies in the world and particularly and primarily those bastions in the reign of evil. That the "gates of Hell" Jesus pronounces indicate that the church is a offensive, not defensive, posture as gates are defensive structures.

I must confess that in reading I was inclined to be in agreement as many of the same thinkers that Myers riffs upon have influenced me also—Walter Wink, Robert Farrar Capon, Greg Boyd, NT Wright, etc... So as I read, I frequently nodded my head in agreement. –GN Trifanaff

The book is well written, easy to understand, organized and consistent thoughts. It rightfully makes the reader at least think about things as... is "the way we have always done it" necessarily the Biblical or Christ-like way, or is it in fact very sinful?! I would recommend the book for pastors and church officers; those who have the most moving-and-shaking clout to implement changes, or keep things the same. –Joel M. Wilson

Purchase the eBook for $4.99
Purchase the Paperback for $8.99

Adventures in Fishing (for Men)

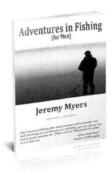

Adventures in Fishing (for Men) is a satirical look at evangelism and church growth strategies.

Using fictional accounts from his attempts to become a world-famous fisherman, Jeremy Myers shows how many of the evangelism and church growth strategies of today do little to actually reach the world for Jesus Christ.

Adventures in Fishing (for Men) pokes fun at some of the popular evangelistic techniques and strategies endorsed and practiced by many Christians in today's churches. The stories in this book show in humorous detail how little we understand the culture that surrounds us or how to properly reach people with the Gospel of Jesus Christ. The story also shows how much time, energy, and money goes into evangelism preparation and training with the end result being that churches rarely accomplish any actual evangelism.

Reviews from Amazon

I found *Adventures in Fishing (For Men)* quite funny! Jeremy Myers does a great job shining the light on some of the more common practices in Evangelism today. His allegory gently points to the foolishness that is found within a system that takes the preaching of the Gospel and tries reduce it to a simplified formula. A formula that takes what should be an organic, Spirit led experience and turns it into a gospel that is nutritionally benign.

If you have ever EE'd someone you may find Meyer's book offensive, but if you have come to the place where you realize that Evangelism isn't a matter of a script and checklists, then you might benefit from this light-hearted peek at Evangelism today. –Jennifer L. Davis

Purchase the eBook for $0.99

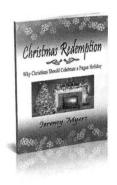

Christmas Redemption: Why Christians Should Celebrate a Pagan Holiday

Christmas Redemption looks at some of the symbolism and traditions of Christmas, including gifts, the Christmas tree, and even Santa Claus and shows how all of these can be celebrated and enjoyed by Christians as a true and accurate reflection of the Gospel.

Though Christmas used to be a pagan holiday, it has been redeemed by Jesus.

If you have been told that Christmas is a pagan holiday and is based on the Roman festival of Saturnalia, or if you have been told that putting up a Christmas tree is idolatrous, or if you have been told that Santa Claus is Satanic and teaches children to be greedy, then you must read this book! In it, you will learn that all of these Christmas traditions have been redeemed by Jesus and are good and healthy ways of celebrating the truth of the Gospel and the grace of Jesus Christ.

Reviews from Amazon

Too many times we as Christians want to condemn nearly everything around us and in so doing become much like the Pharisees and religious leaders that Jesus encountered.

I recommend this book to everyone who has concerns of how and why we celebrate Christmas.

I recommend it to those who do not have any qualms in celebrating but may not know the history of Christmas.

I recommend this book to everyone, no matter who or where you are, no matter your background or beliefs, no matter whether you are young or old. –David H.

Very informative book dealing with the roots of our modern Christmas traditions. The Biblical teaching on redemption is excellent! Highly recommended. –Tamara

Finally, an educated writing about Christmas traditions. I have every book Jeremy Myers has written. His writings are fresh and truthful. –Retlaw "Steadfast"

Purchase the eBook for $0.99

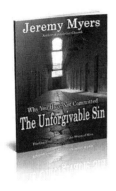

Why You Have not Committed the Unforgivable Sin: Finding Forgiveness for the Worst of Sins

Are you afraid that you have committed the unforgivable sin?

In this book, you will learn what this sin is and why you have not committed it. After surveying the various views about blasphemy against the Holy Spirit and examining Matthew 12:31-32, you will learn what the sin is and how it is committed.

As a result of reading this book, you will gain freedom from the fear of committing the worst of all sins, and learn how much God loves you!

Reviews from Amazon

This book addressed things I have struggled and felt pandered to for years, and helped to bring wholeness to my heart again. –Natalie Fleming

You must read this book. Forgiveness is necessary to see your blessings. So if you purchase this book, [you will have] no regrets. –Virtuous Woman

Jeremy Myers covers this most difficult topic thoroughly and with great compassion. –J. Holland

Good study. Very helpful. A must read. I like this study because it was an in depth study of the scripture. –Rose Knowles

Excellent read and helpful the reader offers hope for all who may be effected by this subject. He includes e-mails from people, [and] is very thorough. –Richie

Purchase the eBook for $4.99
Purchase the Paperback for $5.99

Skeleton Church: A Bare-Bones Definition of Church

The church has a skeleton which is identical in all types of churches. Unity and peace can develop in Christianity if we recognize this skeleton as the simple, bare-bones definition of church. But when we focus on the outer trappings—the skin, hair, and eye color, the clothes, the muscle tone, and other outward appearances—division and strife form within the church.

Let us return to the skeleton church and grow in unity once again.

Reviews from Amazon

My church gathering is struggling to break away from traditions which keep us from following Jesus into the world. Jeremy's book lends encouragement and helpful information to groups like us. –Robert A. White

I worried about buying another book that aimed at reducing things to a simple minimum, but the associations of the author along with the price gave me reason to hope and means to see. I really liked this book. First, because it wasn't identical to what other simple church people are saying. He adds unique elements that are worth reading. Second, the size is small enough to read, think, and pray about without getting lost. –Abel Barba

In *Skeleton Church*, Jeremy Myers makes us rethink church. For Myers, the church isn't a style a worship, a row of pews, or even a building. Instead, the church is the people of God, which provides the basic skeletal structure of the church. The muscles, parts, and flesh of the church are how we carry Jesus' mission into our own neighborhoods in our own unique ways. This eBook will make you see the church differently. –Travis Mamone

This book gets back to the basics of the New Testament church—who we are as Christians and what our perspective should be in the world we live in today. Jeremy cuts away all the institutional layers of a church and gets to the heart of our purpose as Christians in the world we live in and how to affect the people around us with God heart and view in mind. Not a physical church in mind. It was a great book and I have read it twice now. –Vaughn Bender

Purchase the eBook for $0.99

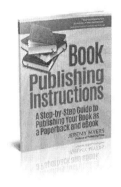

Book Publishing Instructions: A Step-by-Step Guide to Publishing Your Book as a Paperback and eBook

The dirty little secret of the publishing industry is that authors don't really need publishing companies any longer. If you want to get published, you can!

This book gives you everything you need to take your unfinished manuscript and get it into print and into the hands of readers. It shows you how to format your manuscript for printing as a paperback and preparing the files for digital eReaders like the Kindle, iPad, and Nook.

This book provides tips and suggestions for editing and typesetting your book, inserting interior images, designing a book cover, and even marketing your book so people buy it and read it. Detailed descriptions of what to do are accompanied by screenshots for each step. Additional tools, tips, and websites are also provided which will help get your book published.

If you have a book idea, you need to read this book.

Reviews from Amazon

I self-published my first book with the "assistance" of a publishing company. In the end I was extremely unhappy for various reasons ... Jeremy Myers' book ... does not try to impress with all kinds of "learned quotations" but gets right to the thrust of things, plain and simple. For me this book will be a constant companion as I work on a considerable list of books on Christian doctrines. Whether you are a new aspiring author or one with a book or so behind you, save yourself much effort and frustration by investing in this book. –Gerrie Malan

This book was incredibly helpful. I am in the process of writing my first book and the info in here has really helped me go into this process with a plan. I now realize how incredibly naive I was about what goes into publishing a book, yet instead of feeling overwhelmed, I now feel prepared for the task. Jeremy has laid out the steps to every aspect of publishing step by step as though they were recipes in a cook book. From writing with Styles and using the Style guide to incorporating images and page layouts, it is all there and will end up saving you hours of time in the editing phase. –W. Rostoll

Purchase the eBook for $9.99
Purchase the Paperback for $14.99

The Lie – A Short Story

When one billion people disappear from earth, what explanation does the president provide? Is he telling the truth, or exposing an age-old lie?

This fictional short story contains his televised speech.

Have you ever wondered what the antichrist will say when a billion people disappear from planet earth at the rapture? Here is a fictional account of what he might say.

Purchase the eBook for $0.99

Made in the USA
San Bernardino, CA
09 January 2019